CULTIVATING FLOWS

HOW IDEAS BECOME THRIVING ORGANIZATIONS

HERMAN WAGTER & JEAN M. RUSSELL

Published by:
Triarchy Press
Axminster, England

info@triarchypress.net
www.triarchypress.net

Distributed in North America by ISBS
www.isbs.com

A catalogue record for this book is available from the British Library.

Print ISBN: 978-1-909470-98-9
ePub ISBN: 978-1-909470-99-6

Set in Minion Pro.

Cover illustration: Collage of Sputnik blueprint by the authors with artwork by Hava Gurevich.

We would like to thank the original contributors to this book, who gave us their thoughts and essays to build upon:

Anne Caspari
Arthur Brock
Balázs László Karafiáth
Brian Robertson
Christelle Van Ham
Daniel Mezick
Frits Hermans
Deanna Zandt
Eve Simon
Heather Vescent
Howard Silverman
Jon Husband
Kevin Jones
Kevin Marks
Mamading Ceesay
Mark Finnern
Mushin Schilling
Nadia El-Imam
Nathaniel James
Robin Chase
Sofia Bustamante
Thomas John McLeish
Ton van Asseldonk
Valdis Krebs

We would like to acknowledge the generous participation, assistance, and insight of: Nilofer Merchant, Benjamin Ellis, Matthew Schutte, Martin Geddes, Steve Kammen, Damien Brown, Travis Wellman, Manar Hussain, and Ashley Dara Dotz.

And we also thank the generous and inspired contribution of Ayman Sawaf to begin this project, David Isenberg for connecting us, our editor Andrew Carey for pushing us to write clearly, and Nico Anten and the Connekt foundation for many practical examples.

Herman Wagter and Jean Russell

CONTENTS

PART ONE:

HOW SOCIAL FLOWS WORK AND WHY THEY MATTER

INTRODUCTION

Perceiving Flows

J *Flying between San Francisco and Chicago regularly, I watch the change in scenery below. I don't know what you see when you are that high up, but what I see is the evidence of flows. I see the evidence of tectonic shifts of land, water flows, traffic flows, and people flows.*

Even though we do not see them doing it, we know that information and ideas flow, creating their own tracks. I am curious about how information flows. I am also curious about how one idea flows into another, how they mingle and grow.

At the turn of the 20th century, we tended to have a highly mechanical idea of the world: a world of discrete pieces with a specific function, mounted together, according to a design, to perform a more complex task. A rather static, hierarchical view: every piece has its pre-ordained task, the ensemble performing the same repetitive task. Now in our 21st century, there is a more organic, evolving, interrelated idea of the world. A view of the world as a network of mutual relationships, as a variety of ecosystems with a lot of interdependencies. A view more focused on the flows through relationships.

To make use of this book, we invite you to see the world and your country, company, community, and yourself as being in flow, as being embedded in a set of flows. It is an invitation to a rich and exciting view, one you can never be blind to once you have started to perceive it.

Flow:	1) connected stream of movement
	2) psychological state of engagement

Some human flows pop to mind quickly: the flow of traffic, flows of people through a mall or store, the flow of processes and materials through a factory or construction site. Some flows might be harder to notice: the flow of information through communication networks, the flow of ideas through a community, the flow of productivity in your day or week or year, the flow of gossip in your organization, the flow of awareness and knowledge in your head and body. Yet once you start to notice some flows, you will see more and more of them in everyday life and how they have a profound effect on you and those around you.

Boundary:	a limit, like a membrane that allows some things to pass through and others to be contained or repelled

Perceiving this way requires you to step out of the dichotomy of the "inside" versus the "outside" of the organism or organization you are looking at. This asks you to see the flows through the (artificial) boundary by which the "inside" is defined. A living cell is in some sense a self-contained unit with a permeable skin. At the same time, it can only live and thrive by being in a larger flow, by its relationships with other parts of the organism, by receiving and giving back something else in its relationships. Living cells develop themselves, if their ecosystems become more and more elaborate and complex. The same applies to living beings, as well to organizations. It is the flow in and between cells, people, teams—the relationships—that matter to growth.

Ecosystem:	the flows of living organisms in conjunction with the nonliving components of their environment (things like air, water and mineral soil), interacting as a system

The value of flows isn't just related to their size or volume but to the effect they have on your relationship with your ecosystem. Flows are different from transactions across a boundary where letting something out is losing something. Transactions attempt to be tit-for-tat and zero-sum. With flows, there is no zero-sum goal; rather, they draw other, new, valuable things into the interaction. The flow of people down the street is not just about a transaction, where individuals encounter a seller, hand over money, and walk away with a physical object. The flow of people on the street can also make the street a more desirable location, which brings in business opportunities and invites public space interactions and community development. Yes, transactions can be a piece of it, but transactions are not all that happens.

Zero-Sum:	a game or situation in which whatever is gained by one side is lost by the other

Flows never remain the same: depending on their characteristics, they grow or dwindle, change course, twist and turn, split up, join other flows, and change character over time. But the energy that drives a flow can be channeled to a goal, the direction can be changed, the interaction with other flows enhanced or decreased, the size and reach can be expanded: we can influence flows and their effect and, thereby, our world.

Complicated:	having many parts with fairly clear causal relationships
Complex:	having many parts with unknown or even unknowable relationships
Symmathesy:	what Nora Bateson calls living and learning systems. The distinction between mechanical systems with engineering metaphors and living systems with their learning processes needs clearer language, or we will apply the restrictions of mechanical systems to our understanding of living and learning ones

The exciting question is to go one level up from the "inside" and ask how to influence the flows you identify as important to the development of the ecosystem, and therefore your own chances to grow. How to make a difference by growing or diverting flows? Or how to start a new flow, even if you are part of an existing ecosystem?

In this book, we will talk about Emergent, Networked, Event-Driven (ENE) engagements, the flows in places where there are numerous variables, interconnected agents, and triggering events to navigate. Our examples and case studies often include multiple cooperative partners in an ecosystem, such as ports and other transportation networks, multi-sector partnerships, and community-organization hybrids. These make up complex, coordinated, social productivity flows.

Often this degree of complexity is poorly managed by mechanical means; however, our social brains are well equipped to navigate it. Take for instance how we effortlessly walk in a crowded square. Rather than a rigid, command-and-control, central service calculating all the speeds and paths of all objects in a crowded space and giving orders to all of them, we each act individually upon our neighbor's intention and vice versa. Simulations show that giving each participant a few principles such as 1) stay farther apart than x, 2) yield right-of-way, and 3) maintain slow enough speeds to manage principle 1, is enough to navigate that space. Relationships and interaction are all that is needed to create something complex and wonderful. The scientific terminology describes this as an Emergent, Networked, Event-Driven system: what a name for walking in a crowded square.

> Emergent, Networked, Event-Driven (ENE):
> efforts that come into being through networked connections between entities, and stimulated by a triggering event

Here, we're going to tell you about cultivating social flows—about the theory, about how to spot them, and about how they work in practice. We're also going to share with you, drawing on our own experience and that of many interviewees and colleagues, how you can get involved in designing, structuring, and influencing social flows. This book is a guide to help you implement and practice cultivating social flows.

In this book, you will learn how to notice social flows—of ideas, of governance, of agreements, tokens, and people. You will learn about leading-edge practices in shaping social flows and some dangers to avoid or watch for. You may discover opportunities that you could not see before and find ways to get unstuck or overcome hurdles in your team, organization, or community. You will learn about switching from social functional hierarchy to process hierarchy—it is so difficult to switch to thinking this way, but totally crucial to creating effective social flows. We hope you will learn how to become a designer or even a "hacker" of social technology.

Process Hierarchy:	when agreements and processes enable swarm intelligence rather than requiring a functional hierarchy to command and direct activity
Hacker:	someone who enjoys overcoming obstacles with interesting solutions
Social Technology:	the agreements, forms, relationships, behaviors, laws, and concepts we have developed to create more wealth through improved cooperation

If you want to understand, engage, disrupt, create, innovate, and, best of all, transform, the social flows in organizations and communities, flows that are mediated by people—social flows—then this book is for you. We think those who can most benefit from this work are:

➤ members (and leaders) of a consortium or other multi-stakeholder collaborations

➤ cross-sector collaborators or facilitators

➤ community development innovators, online and offline

➤ organizational design innovators and entrepreneurs

➤ software developers for the above

Our Social Flow Here

We, the authors, have been meeting in cafés across Europe for several years to discuss breakthroughs in our work creating and coordinating social flows as well as insights into how to improve. As these insights were put into practice and seen to be successful, a demand arose for a guide for practitioners. This is it.

Being who we are, we created social flows of our own to generate this book. In the Fall of 2013, we scoured our networks for people who were paying attention to the creation and development of social flows.

Throughout the book, the names of contributors to our inquiry who have essays and interviews on CultivatingFlows.com are shown in bold.

We spoke with social network scientist **Valdis Krebs**, business innovators like **Robin Chase** (Zipcar, Peers Inc.), and systems thinker and writer, **Howard Silverman**. We spoke with storyteller and Creative Director for the award winning Beaconfire Red design studio, **Eve Simon**, and **Ton van Asseldonk**, an economist who applies his knowledge of complexity in event-driven (ENE) systems in practice for his customers. We spoke with social software innovator **Kevin Marks** as well as community development entrepreneurs such as **Sofia Bustamante** and **Mamading Ceesay** at London Creative Labs. We interviewed governance innovator **Brian Robertson** of HolacracyOne. We spoke to futurists like **Heather Vescent** and currency innovators such as **Arthur Brock**. We didn't just talk to engineer-types who work on the tangible technology and design but also to social-types who understand how humans actually work in the real and messy world and who build communities and organizations from that reality. Everyone shared their years of experience and practice in building social flows that work— and lessons from what doesn't.

We wanted to know how they had solved the real problems they faced. We held a retreat to discuss the material that had emerged from the group. Then we held weekly online community calls with an extended group of practitioners to process their insights and wisdom. We organized, synthesized, polished, wrestled with, and chewed on what evolved to become this book and the corresponding website, CultivatingFlows.com (where the essays and interviews live and can continue to grow and evolve).

While we, the authors, hold the vision, the wisdom captured here relies on a community in flow as well as threading out into various resources including books and articles, which we are collecting on the website. This can continue to flow and expand with your participation. This book is your introductory guide and overview; the website holds the expanding resources. Join us at CultivatingFlows.com to contribute your stories and lessons.

Why "Cultivating Social Flows"?

Antifragile:	"Some things benefit from shocks; they thrive and grow when exposed to volatility, randomness, disorder, and stressors and love adventure, risk, and uncertainty. Yet, in spite of the ubiquity of the phenomenon, there is no word for the exact opposite of fragile. Let us call it antifragile. Antifragility is beyond resilience or robustness. The resilient resists shocks and stays the same; the antifragile gets better." [www.fooledbyrandomness.com]

In a world of knowledge and creativity, we can't design a system by breaking it down into many, small, repetitive tasks as if we were working with a machine. We do not control what people do with their minds. We must appeal to them if we are to engage their minds and creativity in the work we are to do together. So how do we engage other beings in work, play, and society? We believe the insights and examples in this book will help give you the tools to pragmatically approach cultivating social flows.

Cultivating Social Flows: Cultivating describes the process and practice of caring for aliveness in an organic system. Cultivating is also associated with evolving culture. Thus cultivating social flows is the care and tending of generative motion and connection for people within an ecosystem.

First we will expand on what we mean by cultivating social flows and why they matter. Then we will look at how they function and why. We will present the guiding framework we use to describe the spectrum of phases that social flows often evolve through—we will explore this framework deeply throughout the book. We will provide tools and techniques born from practicing this work, highlighting potential difficulties we have noticed. We want to enable you to move into practice, so we end each chapter with key concepts or quick guides to cultivating social flows.

H *In this book we introduce the label 'cultivating social flows' for what has become the core of my practice for the last 15 years. My practice is about getting things done, about getting results as a program manager in large complex programs, where many stakeholders, including government agencies, aim to move in a desired direction. Some of it is related to transport and sustainability, some of it to the infrastructure of the Internet (like Fiber-to-the-Home). It was Jean who introduced me to the thinkers and concepts that put a lot more theory and experience behind my practice. I could feed stuff I picked up back into her work, like the difference between control, influence, and nurture which turned out to link into thrivability. She pointed me to theories and experiences, showing me what concepts are applicable. I, in turn, could point Jean to hard, practical applications of these ideas, showing their value in practice. The combination was like opening a door to a new world.*

Many of our conversations since that time share the "Eureka" and "leapfrog effect" moments. Exploring ideas, applying them in practice immediately, feeding back the results in our conversations. The immediate positive outcomes were exhilarating! All this makes me want to jump up and tell anybody who will listen.

Over time we identified the strategies for cultivating social flows that are common to many interesting thinkers and practitioners: thinkers who give structure and depth to ideas we apply intuitively; practitioners who are doing this kind of work, day-in, day-out. We found practical, real-life examples of the application of the ideas, showing what is possible. And we found many who are as hungry as we are for new knowledge, who want to explore more widely, pushing the boundaries of our knowledge and experience.

Please note, we are pragmatists. (Psssst, most books are not written by pragmatists.) This book is the result of our unique partnership. Get your essential learning about what works in practice here! Our work evolved from the insights of on-the-ground practices and not from the often idealized stories of MBA programs backfilling stories to fit a preconceived model.

As pragmatists, we noticed repeatedly the intense interlinking of strategy development and the creation of a social culture fit for implementing that strategy. Without that, as Peter Drucker said and Mark Fields, President of Ford Motor Co., made famous, "*Culture* eats *strategy* for breakfast." We will talk, throughout the book, about ways to weave together strategy and culture.

Social Flows Matter

No doubt, you will have seen the rise of words like swarm, hive, collective intelligence, crowd-this or crowd-that. Much of our flows work leans in the direction of swarms and collective action. Swarm behavior emerges from a large set of individuals, loosely connected by simple interaction rules or principles. There is abundant research on how, for example, flocks of sparrows or starlings perform beautiful dances in the evening sky, or on how ant colonies are highly effective in finding food in any environment. A handful of simple interaction rules used by every participant is enough to let amazing behavior emerge. Yet if the actors are alone, without interaction, the observed collective behavior is absent.

Upper level flows:	the movement of the whole, as in the flow of traffic as a whole
Lower level flows:	the movement of any given individual, as in the flow of a single car

Collective behavior can be seen as an upper level flow. In society, we can identify similar flows that emerge from masses of individual behavior. This we call a social flow, as opposed to the flow of water or the dance of a flock of sparrows. We distinguish it from other swarm behaviors because we know individual humans can be conscious of their flows, create and adjust the simple rules governing the swarms they create, and make choices about how they participate.

Swarms don't usually have single leaders who maintain leadership. Swarms have fluid leadership. Swarm leaders temporarily guide direction. For example, with birds, a bird that flies far from the flock might not inspire followership in the flock. Instead it may be the second or even third bird, who follows the first, thereby inspiring the shift in the flock. No bird by position or authority sets the course for any other bird in the flock. Leadership changes between the birds in the flock, while each bird follows simple principles. Ducks fly in a V, rotating who takes point. Through this book, we will cover various ways leadership plays out in social flows and what role you can play in being leaderful.

Leadership:	providing guidance and direction—while leadership in command-and-control domains focuses coercing action through power and transactions, leadership in social flows relies more on compelling narrative, demonstration, and clarity of mutual benefits

If you have traveled, you may have noticed that traffic, while generally having similar rules most places you go, may have very different behavior. Like other social flows, the mechanisms may be similar in different situations but the culture and consciousness of the local area may shift behavior significantly.

In a social flow the individuals are humans who may be aware of the collective behavior they are part of. They may agree with the flow and its perceived result, or disagree and actively oppose it. It implies a tension held between "me" and "we" within social flows. As we will show, culture is a key component in managing this tension.

J *I didn't think the integration of strategy and culture was unusual until someone else remarked on it. I was facilitating a strategy retreat for a growing startup in Canada. The primary goal of the client was to develop a strategy for moving forward with their mission. The secondary goal was to build team coherence with the new additions. I invited each person in attendance, having considered what they knew of the project, to say what the risk of failure was, from their perspective. Each person took about 15 minutes to present their primary risk. Then I asked each person to come from the other side of the flipchart to present what the organization could do to address the risk they had just presented—*

because often that person was best qualified to solve the problem they had noticed.

Afterwards, the clients wrote a testimonial: "...neither of us have ever seen anyone link creative team building to organizational outcomes as deeply as Jean Russell did for us. Her workshop facilitation for us was geared towards actually doing work."

After that workshop, the startup had a more rigorous strategy. More than that, the opportunity to address their biggest concern meant that the people involved were more committed. A culture of frank honesty along with a "who names the problem, leads in solving the problem" culture emerged.

Culture:	the customs, traditions and values of a group—culture shows up through design, language, and beliefs as well as rituals and other behaviors and social processes

Effective social flows emerge from a dynamic harmony between strategy and culture. Culture is not an add-on handled by HR doing unrelated-to-work team building. Rather, culture should be seen as an anthropologist sees it: written and unwritten sets of social protocols and behaviors, together creating a force by which strategy and operations develop and maintain coherence.

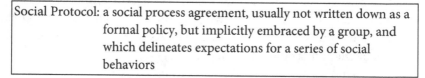

Social Protocol:	a social process agreement, usually not written down as a formal policy, but implicitly embraced by a group, and which delineates expectations for a series of social behaviors

Culture shows up within the implicit and explicit governance of a collection of participants. Governance is not only the policies but also the norms, beliefs, and language of a group, as they get reinforced through participation.

Where strategy is not aligned with the existing culture, we face an uphill battle. Where culture does not embrace strategy, flows are stifled. When they are aligned, culture and strategy can have lunch together.

When we cultivate culture so that it serves our direction for action, the degree to which it comes alive and self-maintains, we call coherence. So throughout the book we will talk less about culture in the abstract and much more about the kind of culture we desire—one that has coherence.

Coherence

We have chosen to use the word coherence to describe the various aspects of desirable culture that operate in the social flow design process. Coherence describes this desired meeting point between behavior and strategy.

Coherence is why a diverse and changing group of people keeps on contributing to a shared purpose. Coherence welcomes diversity, is inclusive for everyone who feels in sync, and contributes to, and is geared for, natural growth.

Three aspects of culture that we have identified and that we call Coherence, are as follows:

Narrative: The narrative tells what the purpose is, why we want to achieve the purpose, how to get there from where we are now, what roles there are in the journey, what options we have, and what our strengths are.

Motives: Understanding the variety of primary motives people have, and what that means for their willingness to contribute and how to adapt to that, is essential. For example, we need to approach social flows knowing that those attracted to early phases of inspiration may not be motivated to do the detailed structure building or bug fixes on technology. Part of cultivating social flows is opening spaces for people as they are, with their own personal motives, interests, and abilities, so they can fit into the flow appropriately.

Governance: The implicit and explicit rules we apply to ourselves and our joint activities which facilitate cooperation. Governance provides a predictable system of what a group needs: care, safety, and security. Working on governance means we can begin to answer questions like: How can we create safe and nurturing connections that are able to innovate and grow? How can we defend ourselves against bad actors inside and outside? How can we make decisions?

While these all influence the development of coherence in each phase, we will focus on one or another as we go through the phases, as well as including ideas and practices for flow leadership.

Social Organism:	the collective as a unit, held together by a narrative and the motives of the participants, bound by a semipermeable membrane of governance

The Case for Social Flows

Money talks, so it is said. But is it the only or most effective way to get people to invest their energy and wisdom in a purpose, to arrange mutually beneficial relationships and exchanges, or influence choices?

No, it is not the only method, nor the most effective.

Our literature, plays and movies (starting at a young age with "A Christmas Carol") are full of stories that convey the same message: if you value money over relationships, you are a poor schmuck who doesn't get life. We are social animals by nature.

Borrowing something from your neighbor implies not only that you will lend something out as well, when asked. It also implies that you have a relationship that lasts over time; that you will look after each other. Borrowing and lending back and forth, over time, we are never quite clear if we have fully reciprocated. We resist the feeling that we may still owe our neighbor a return favor and yet, in that unclosable gap, our relationship blossoms and trust grows. It is the start of a community, which is highly valued.

Borrowing something from your neighbor and paying him money implies that you expect nothing afterwards. No enduring relationship, please. Bringing flowers or chocolate or wine worth $20 to friends who invited you to dinner at their home sends the message that you value their friendship highly, while leaving a $50 bill ends the friendship. It is hard to find anyone who thinks barn-raising by the Amish is silly because they do not pay each other; quite the opposite. We intuitively understand the relationship of reciprocity. The Golden Rule is globally recognized.

> Reciprocity: positively or negatively connoted responses of individuals reflecting back the actions of others—acting on the golden rule to do unto others as you would have them do unto you.

Paying for something conveys the message that you do NOT want a relationship with the person you pay. The accounting is very clear in a way that "clears the debt" so to speak. And the clearing of the debt can mean the relationship does not need to continue. Thus money can stop highly valued social flows, if you are not careful.

The common business and political "wisdom," however, is that financial incentives are needed to make people do the thing you want in organizations or in society. So we see bonuses, fines, tax credits, and many more monetized incentives and punishments being introduced time and again, even repeatedly after the failure of the previous scheme has been forgotten. Numerous studies by behavioral economists show that not only do financial incentives lead to poorer decision-making, but social incentives can be a lot more persuasive, longer lasting, and less costly financially, than pure financial incentives.

Sometimes financial incentives have side effects that pervert the goal: the famous "cobra effect", where the unintended consequences of a solution actually make the problem worse. The recent financial crisis is rife with modern examples of this phenomenon.

Money as a motivator in work is more limited than many people imagine: Daniel Pink explains in an "RSA Animate"[1] how several studies commissioned by stalwart institutions like the FED show that financial incentives only work in simple manual jobs. As soon as there is any cognitive effort needed, financial incentives no longer have the desired effect and may even cause the opposite. It turns out most people are much more motivated by Mastery, Purpose, and Autonomy than by Money (provided they have enough money to sustain a normal life).

One could argue, therefore, that throwing *only* financial incentives at a problem equals intellectual laziness: easy to design, but at the price of being costly and at best partially effective, if not counterproductive. Social flows, as in interactions in a network of people, are more difficult to design, but they can generate much more value.

Let's take an example from the business arena, resulting in increased efficiency.

Use Case: Gain-sharing

Container shipping has made the transport of goods over large distances incredibly cheap. A standard 40ft container can hold $67m^3$ at a weight of 30 tonnes, and will be shipped from China to the USA by sea for a couple of thousand dollars. The common practice is that the shipping companies own the containers that are provided. Which means that you have to take back the empty container to the port after you have emptied the full one (import), or pick up an empty container at the port before you can load it with cargo and take the full container to the port again (export).

---

[1] You'll find links to any books, films, articles and other resources that are underlined at the website: CultivatingFlows.com.

When a port is connected by inland waterways, barges are a popular method for transporting batches of containers to an inland terminal near a concentration of factories and warehouses.

One terminal owner in the Netherlands noticed that more and more he was taking as many empty containers back to the port as he was picking up empty in the port to bring back to his terminal, all in the same day or week, all on behalf of various principals, and with different shipping companies. What if he could reuse an import container which had just been emptied? There might be a neighbor just waiting for an empty container to fill it with cargo for export. That could halve the transport costs for inland shipping and make his terminal much more attractive.

The trouble was that it required a complex dance between parties who had no relationship with one another. Reusing a container requires at a minimum that both parties (import and export) book at the same shipping company. The shipping company has to agree with the swap of the uniquely identified container. The timing has to be right. And, last but not least, how to divide the profit resulting from the reduced transport costs?

The solution was to engage a social flow.

The inland terminal owner invited his biggest customers to dinner and explained the potential if they could agree to cooperate. They agreed, after exploring various options, that it would only work if there was trust, easy opt-in or opt-out, and if everyone benefited.

In this new rental arrangement, the trust part is secured by an informal regular meeting of the stakeholders to check on how the arrangement is working, to discuss governance issues, and to remove irritations. With regard to opt-in/opt-out: any new company can join as long as they accept the (unwritten) rules; anybody can leave if they feel they need to. The financial benefits are divided equally between the two parties exchanging containers and the terminal that does the matchmaking.

Operationally, the partners tell the terminal in advance what transport they foresee in the near future. The terminal makes matches and helps select the shipping company they both will use.

After a while over 80% of the containers were re-used, a massive saving in money and emissions made possible by a creating a new social flow.

> Why do we consider this a social flow instead of "just" cost-saving? Because other terminals have tried setting up a small company dedicated to doing the exchange, charging money for the service. They failed. The key difference is that relationships built upon mutual trust between individuals made the flow possible, and led to monetary benefits. When gain-sharing was approached initially as a monetary challenge (how to divide the spoils) it failed.

Social Era

Over the last decade a lot of companies have proven that conversations as opposed to pure monetary transactions can deliver huge value. Nilofer Merchant authored a series of articles on this observation under the title "The Social Era" in the _Harvard Business Review_ blog, which became a book, _11 Rules for Creating Value in the #SocialEra_.

Merchant shows how much value is created for companies today by social flows compared to a decade or two ago. She writes, "Because it has shown up in bits and pieces, via freemium models, crowdsourcing, online communities, virtual workforces, social networks, and so on, it is easy to miss how much the overall context has changed for the way value is created."

Merchant importantly shows how this new Social Era includes way more than just using social media and applying the latest marketing strategies. In the Social Era, companies do things very differently from the post WWII industrial model.

In the old industrial model, size—as in number of staff and assets—was the path to efficiency and cost advantage, and size brought access to more financial capital. In the Social Era, infrastructure and operational costs are significantly streamlined, fitting into a vast external network that aids in creating value; and transaction costs are minimized to near zero by applying the power of the Internet and IT. The size and quality of your relationship network becomes the key to success.

In the old model, we see Porter's Value Chain—a linear approach to supply chains that push products to markets. In the Social Era, markets are conversations, as _The Cluetrain Manifesto_ suggested fifteen years ago. A Social Era company takes in feedback from customers to inform every part of its business, enabling each person involved to act as a sense organ of the organization. Engaging with people outside the company is about developing ongoing relationships, not just transactions. And this means a lot more sharing, which makes the organization more vulnerable and less predictable, and attracts valuable relationships, rather than telling/ broadcasting like the old media forms encouraged. We know this as the push model. Innovation in the Social Era is not just better products at lower prices. It is innovations in organizational design and process—Social Flows.

In her blog post, Nilofer writes,

> *Collaborating with people through shared purpose creates advantage because it allows everyone to work towards a shared goal. When people know the purpose of an organization, they don't need to check in or get permission to take the next step, they can just do it. When people know the purpose, they are not waiting to be told what to do. With shared purpose, alignment happens without coordination costs. Shared purpose makes customers and team-members more than transactions and payroll recipients. It allows us to "tear down that wall" between who is "in" or "outside" the firm creating a more permeable organization which unleashes the inherently collaborative nature of work — like a herd of gazelles running leaderless, daringly, across a plain. This is the foundational principle of the social era.*

We believe that this value extends itself beyond companies: the same value can be found for government institutions, communities and social institutions as described by economist Elinor Ostrom and her associates. All of these organizational forms can benefit from valuable, meaningful, and purposeful social flows.

The challenge is to resist the temptation of the simple financial control description of how the world interacts, to resist introducing naive mechanical pushes and pulls based on (only) financial rewards, to invest the intellectual energy in designing for rich social flows. It starts with looking for the flows that drive the conversations, that enable sharing.

What We Offer in This Book

Part One paints the picture of what social flows are, why they matter, and some tools for understanding their mechanics. After our introduction, we provide a use case of a social flow, Lean and Green, making clear by example what we will be exploring in the book. Before going into the chapters on practice, we provide some background in Chapter 2. One of the core models is the contemporary view of what a network is and how it functions, which we will cover with some other tools for understanding social flows. Some readers will be familiar with the content of this chapter, while for others it will be new ground. You might scan the chapter and use the concluding key concepts or quick guide as a checklist to be sure you have the foundational knowledge to move forward, or you can swim in the links and connections, exploring the foundation and related ideas before moving forward.

Reviewing our case studies and their approaches to cultivating social flows, we noticed that phases can be identified. These are not clearly defined phases with abrupt starts and stops; they are broad ways of seeing what is happening, which, in practice, turns out to be messy, iterative, and interdependent. For convenience, we have untangled them for you to perceive the elements. In your own practice the boundaries between these phases will most likely be murky.

The phases we noticed by zooming out and looking for patterns across numerous efforts are: Reframing and Navigating (described in Part Two), Operationalizing (Part Three), and Evaluating and Iterating (Part Four). Within each phase there are practices that focus on building coherence. We have teased these apart a bit; however, again, in real world implementations, the structures and the social elements tangle together.

Reframing and Navigating

In Part Two, we look at the early seeds of an innovation. Reframing builds the dream of a new and attractive future. Reframing the territory creates a new understanding of what is possible. That space might be a mental space, an organizational space, or a relational space. It breaks the mental boundaries given by our existing internal models of the world. We see and understand what something is in a different way. It is like seeing a heat map instead of a topographical map in the way it transforms what is seen without changing what is there.

Reframes build a dream of a better future, by using this new space to get there. Entering the new possibility space, we want to fill it with a network of people, with new relationships. In reframing, we seek to connect people, ideas, and create relationships. But who or what interacts with whom or what? What does that generate or make possible? The new relationships generate new options for action, using the available possibility space. The more options the better, allowing for the development of a rich set of scenarios and strategies to operationalize the dream. So Navigating follows Reframing, where we explore and make maps to help others navigate the new understanding. In Navigating we look at what scenarios or possibilities might arise that would be useful to us and others. We mentally play out possibilities and map those opportunities for others.

Still, reframing and navigating mostly just get us to an adjacent possibility, nascent and small scale, incubating under the benevolent regard of co-conspirators of the idea—our allies. To scale and extend our reach in time and space, we need to operationalize the idea with more people.

Operationalizing

Once we have a reframe and we see how we will navigate it together, including the scenario to achieve the next (or first) step in implementation, and contingency plans are prepared, then answers to tough questions of scaling it out must be generated.

In Part Three, we explore the form for growth, processes for flow, and how to manage all this, as well as the support tools needed to operationalize ideas at scale. How does the new way of seeing and the new architecture or design get implemented? What are the flows within it? And how is it self-regulating (how does power work within it)? We create teams, tribes, and communities. We turn the new options and new relationships into actions, for instance by adding tools to facilitate making a choice (navigation of options), or by introducing participation options like alternative currencies or tokens, or creating governance. Finally, the rubber meets the road. We build forms, flows, and tools to support the social flow.

Evaluating and Iterating

Social flows are complex and adaptive. What worked yesterday may not work tomorrow. We have to keep evaluating and build on what we learn. We create a prototype and keep iterating. Creating learning systems means that evaluation and iteration become part of the process. To deal with rapid change and complexity we design anti-fragile solutions that can adapt and learn. In Part Four, we share processes for evaluation and iteration, including assessment questions and how to think about instrumentation for evaluation.

Prototype:	a sample, model, or release of a product built to test a concept or process or to act as a thing to be replicated or learned from (historically, it was considered a first attempt, but now, given that conditions may be in constant flux, the best that may be done is iterations of prototypes with no finished, static pattern)

Key Concepts in this Chapter

Perceiving Flows
- Flow
- Boundary
- Ecosystem
- Zero-Sum
- Symmathesy
- Complicated
- Complex
- Emergent, Networked, Event-Driven (ENE)
- Process Hierarchy
- Hacker
- Social Technology

Why Cultivating Social Flows
- Antifragile
- Cultivating Social Flows

Social Flows Matter
- Upper Level Flows
- Lower Level Flows
- Leadership
- Culture
- Social Process
- Social Protocol

Coherence
- Narratives
- Motives
- Governance
- Social Organism

The Case for Social Flows
- Reciprocity
- Gain-sharing

Social Era

This Book
- Reframing and Navigating
- Operationalizing
- Evaluating and Iterating

CHAPTER 1:

USE CASE: LEAN AND GREEN

H In 2007 I was asked by the Connekt foundation to assist in a government-sponsored program which aimed to achieve a reduction in CO_2 emissions from freight transport. The following describes the challenge and intervention.

A number of studies had shown that the potential for improvement was huge, even without investing in low-emission technology like hydrogen or electric trucks. The driving style of the driver and good maintenance (like tire pressure) are examples of easy wins. The other big potential saving was in optimization of the total logistics network, by combining supply chains, leading to fuller trucks and ships. The projected CO_2 emission reductions were 30% or more, and most of the emission reductions would also lead to cost reductions, as less fuel and fewer resources would be used.

Yet relatively few trucking companies or shippers took decisive action. When interviewed, many gave reasons why they couldn't do it singlehandedly. They said they had almost no control. They only reigned over a very limited part of the system, so they could not be responsible for the collective inaction. Competition was fierce, limiting their ability to invest, so only if someone regulated prices or reduced competition could they make enough money to buy better technology. If everyone moved, they could move too; but only if someone else would start. If science were to invent a silver bullet they would use it: meaning the same truck for the same price with no emission. And so on.

The challenge was to create a movement that would break the stalemate.

As the traditional approaches (warning of impending doom if we did not reduce emissions) had already been tried, we had to invent something new—we needed a reframe. We decided to take a positive approach:

1. *demonstrate that sustainability is not an unachievable ideal but simply the combination of lower emissions and a better performing operation, delivering more bang for the buck.*

2. *focus on the front runners who already see the potential, and ignore the curmudgeons.*

3. *create a demand-driven program, guided by the early adopters and front runners.*

We coined the catchy name Lean and Green. Lean and Green expressed concisely the combination of more value/less waste and lower emissions. The next step was to create a community that collectively articulated the shared goals, determine how to move forward as a group, and take ownership of the movement.

The Lean and Green reframing brought the reward back into taking action. It was, by design, aimed at the frontrunners, the ones already toying with the idea, to galvanize them.

A simple method to operationalize the reframe was designed and tested, a motivational reward system was added, and, with the help of government, the reframe was scaled up successfully in practice.

Operationally we started to attract companies to make the effort to receive an Award (a Current-See—see p.148). Any shipping or transport company that made a solid, audited plan to reduce their CO_2 emissions by at least 20% within five years and make that goal part of their official policy would receive the Lean and Green Award. Members received some coaching on how to plan the reduction, with emphasis on reducing costs in parallel: lower fuel costs, less idle capacity, more loads, and so on. The mantra was that only changes that improve your competitiveness are sustainable over the long run: Lean and Green.

The award was nothing more (or less) than publicity and recognition by their peers in a ceremony, and the right to carry a huge sticker on their trucks.

Much to our delight, the idea really got traction after the first companies started to drive around with big stickers. They reported back that the simple target, the public policy statement, the need to incorporate multiple departments to develop the plan, and the feedback on how they were doing energized the company. The direct results in cost reduction caught the eye of the CFO. They started to exchange best practices with each other. The big sticker was a talking point with peers, and after a while got the attention of potential customers.

The growth and success created its own reaction, such as copycats and competition. Some big multinational corporations who are used to top-down decision structures and managed projects did not like the organic growth and pace of the development, and decided to start something similar but managed. Some trade organizations wanted to have more connection with their core membership. In other countries governments started similar programs.

The early frontrunners asked for one or more next levels, so they could differentiate themselves from late entrants; some even wanted a goal of zero emissions. They asked for more absolute benchmarking, so as to be able to compare their performance and use it in purchasing decisions. There was a growing focus on the difficult issue of cooperation between competitors.

Today, Lean and Green is one of the most successful programs in Europe for both shippers and transportation companies, and a thought leader on how to incorporate sustainability into operational excellence. The core strength during these years has been the community that feels ownership of the program.

Reframing does not have to be aimed at pleasing everybody, at first. The reframe resulted in moving more than just the early adopters. It created a flow that eventually would draw in even the curmudgeons. If there are strong supporters who see the benefit for themselves, the reframe will be adopted.

CHAPTER 2:

BEHIND THE CURTAIN—HOW SOCIAL FLOWS WORK

Social Flows have a number of key characteristics and it is helpful to understand these characteristics before we move into practice. Even though some of you will be deeply knowledgeable about many of these areas already, it might be helpful to check our terms in any case. The following concepts are some of our key assumptions in perceiving and cultivating social flows.

Networks

The word "network" has permeated our language. Decades ago most professionals talked about things like structure, hierarchy, functions, departments, and business units. Everything had to be given a specific place, and order gave people the sense of a designed piece, of an "optimum" design that needed only routine maintenance once a state of equilibrium had been attained.

Now we talk much more often about relationships and describe our world as a network: a network of corporations that constitute a supply network, a network of professionals, a social network. The word "network" has connotations of many relationships, of quickly adapting to new dynamics, of richness and complexity, of exchanging information which benefits all, of "the sum is more than the collection of parts." Finally, the word "network" suggests that "as part of our context and wider environment, we can go further than we can go alone." A network is something we are part of: it extends beyond the boundaries of our own organization and is in constant flux.

The idea of networks and flows gives us the opportunity to "design" them. Well, the word design would imply an engineering mindset. In practice it is more like cultivating a garden, a new variety of flowers or fruit. It is about dealing with life instead of matter.

Flow Interactions Seen as a Network

To understand social flows so we can cultivate them, it helps to look at some basic network science first. Social interactions, relationships, and transactions between people can be modeled as a network. The nodes of the network are individuals, the relationships between them are depicted as connections between nodes.

Social Network:	a network of social interactions and relationships: "An axiom of the social network approach to understanding social interaction is that social phenomena should be primarily conceived and investigated through the properties of relations between and within units, instead of the properties of these units themselves." [Wikipedia]

As Albert-László Barabási and others have shown, the natural development of this kind of social network will result in a particular topology, because it can continue to extend infinitely. Many nodes have a relatively small number of relationships, while a few nodes have many relationships. Some people are extremely well connected, one would say. The exciting part of this discovery is that the well-connected people play a vital role in making the network accessible and navigable.

Trust Beyond Dunbar's Number

A human can only intimately know and trust a very limited number of people. Dunbar's number is often cited as a natural limit. According to that theory, we build and maintain mental models of others. These models help us to understand and predict someone's emotions, desires, and drives, and help us to estimate how far we can trust the other. The theory says that a human can keep approximately 150 individuals and their relationships (Dunbar's number) in mind, which is very limited compared to the size of society. As trust is one of the core ingredients of relationships, and therefore of social flows, this limit could have been crippling.

But we found a bypass for it so we can deal with billions of relationships. Trust-by-proxy, in combination with well-connected people, is the means to overcome that limit to a large extent.

Trust-by-proxy means that you trust someone else's judgment and character. For example, Kris is someone you know very well, someone you respect and trust, someone whose judgment has proven to be reliable on the topic at hand. Most likely close friends of Kris will have the same type of character and morals as Kris, or they would not be friends. As a default, it is relatively safe to trust friends of Kris on face value, as if they were Kris. And maybe even a friend of a friend of Kris. Of course this has limits and fails some of the time, yet it helps connect people every day. The opposite is true as well: you will be biased against the friends of someone you dislike and distrust.

H *We have more sensory equipment to assess trust than you might imagine. You need only a fraction of a second when entering a room to sense the "atmosphere": is there hostility, joy or grief? Biologists have wondered for a long time why we humans (unlike most other animals) have 3 color receptors in our eyes, of which two are very close to each other in spectral sensitivity. The answer, according to* Mark Changizi, *is that this particular combination gives us a high sensitivity for reading variation in skin tones created by changes in the blood flow—even though we have remarkably few words to describe skin tones precisely. Your face shows in this way if you are agitated or not inside, if you are poised for aggression or not, if you are scared or not. Our eyes allow us to sense whether the words uttered match the state of the body. Masks and high levels of makeup hide this skin tone: we see the faces of geishas as being unreadable. It does not matter if someone has a Caucasian skin tone or an African skin tone. The spectral characteristics of both skin tones are much more alike than we might think them to be and we still can "read" the other's state. It only takes a few weeks to recalibrate your senses from one tone to another, which might explain the high levels of mistrust when people with different skin tones first meet each other.*

Well-connected people shorten the communication distance between any two individuals dramatically. They cause the famous "6 handshakes" or "6 degrees of separation" phenomenon: you can reach anybody in a world of 7 billion people within 6 handshakes. The math is simple: if I know someone who knows a 1,000 people, who knows someone who knows 1,000 people, and so on, we would potentially reach a billion people by the third handshake if there were no overlap between the networks. Even with only 150 instead of 1,000 connections you go beyond 6 billion in 5 handshakes.

If you know and trust a person who is very well connected, you may quickly find through her or him someone who you do not know but most likely can be trusted. Reputation is everything. Many of our emerging social technologies help us navigate trust beyond Dunbar's number.

Social flows ride on social networks.

Self-Interest or Paying Forward

H *I have been told, "experience is what you get by pushing the envelope, wisdom is when you learn from experience to prevent mistakes." Looking back, I would add that wisdom can be conveyed to you by people willing to share their experience, and how they have learned from it. At least that is how I experienced it.*

Early on I became uncomfortable with the one-sidedness of this type of exchange: I could not return the favor. It gave me a sense of becoming indebted to them. When I expressed my uneasiness to someone, their answer was a surprise. "Of course you have to pay back the favor, with interest... by giving similar advice to others, later in your life, twice!" A great deal, from my point of view. I lost count of the number of times I was on the receiving end, so I just keep on giving advice (happily), including the "pay forward clause." It makes me happy to pass on what I have learned.

We often over-simplify the concept of self-interest into economic terms. Here we mean something more nuanced. Humans have motivations for doing what we do. And they may not be the same for everyone. We may feel our self-interest is served if we experience a sense of connection and belonging with others. Or we may feel like we are part of a larger whole and a greater purpose than our own. We may derive meaning from altruism. Or, maybe, we are more motivated by a sense of achievement as we reach some goals we share together. Perhaps we are motivated by a desire to influence the world by changing policies or governance. We can also be motivated by the experience of being in flow states as we develop proficiency in a skill. Self-interest does not have to be about gaining economic value. Mutual self-interest means that we willingly engage in a group or team because we benefit in a way that matters to us.

Many real-life examples can be portrayed as a network of voluntary relationships, with multiple players, and not just two in a simple transaction closing out through reciprocity. The exchanges are not simple one-on-one (bartering), but convoluted and complex, weaving through the network before returning to you. When we design for mutual self-interest, we look at how each party may benefit directly, yes. So, at the meagre, economic level, helping out a friend of a friend might lead to a praise of your character in a time and place you may never be aware of. Something that might make a difference when your name comes up in a conversation, leading to a contact which is very beneficial to you. But we can also look beyond that to pay-it-forward, where a party may feel grateful about what they received, and gift it on to a third party. This forms giving chains, rather than simple reciprocity loops, in our flows.

The loops and chains of contribution can also have time delays, sometimes of extended length. You contribute something to me now, and next month or year, I contribute back or to the whole or to someone else. If there is low trust, the time delays need to be short or mediated by a third entity or process that is trusted. If the trust is high, payback is not accounted for and implicitly has a long window. Imagine your best friend buying you lunch and how soon you may need to buy a lunch for them. If the two of you move to different continents, it might be that the next chance to payback is when their son or daughter comes to visit.

High trust means a long time and/or a long chain is accepted, low trust goes in the direction of tit-for-tat.

High trust allows for "paying forward" not only in bits of wisdom, but also in monetary terms. Some philanthropists have even set up a "forward revolving fund." The loan and interest is not paid "back" but paid "forward" to the next person needing such a loan.

Trust: Personal, Institutional, and Buffer Zones

Trust is a precious good, of high value and scarce. **Valdis Krebs**, in the essay he contributed to this project, explores the value of trust in creating connections. Trust equals proximity in relationships; in a sense it shrinks horizons for each node. For example: the "new" idea is that you can get quality food that you can trust if you bypass the retailers who have dominated the food chain and get it close to home, supporting the local economy. Transactional agreements that are only based on legal documents with absolute strangers do not have the same value as trust based on personal social ties.

Yet sometimes transactional trust, based on institutions, is all we have available to get to the scale needed. Strangers who do not trust each other can exchange and create wealth based on transactions mediated by institutions that they each trust. This makes products and services possible that you could not get otherwise. Institutional trust is, in that case, the only option available. It codifies the mutuality.

Kevin Jones, in his interview for this book, points to the opportunity costs of relying too much on existing personal or organizational trust, pointing out the value of neutral buffer zones. Existing trust relationships are safe, well-known, easy to use. The danger is that you may lull yourself into missing new blood, new ideas, new opportunities from the outside. The value of cross-pollination of ideas across groups is huge. As Alex Pentland describes in _Social Physics: How Good Ideas Spread_, we do not grow good new ideas if we stay in an echo chamber which repeats itself comfortably. The answer is to actively seek new ideas and fresh insights, to seek cross-pollination.

It can be observed in practice how buffer zones and safe areas are created, on purpose, to facilitate "safe cross-pollination." For example: the highest value of a convention or conference lies not in the presentations given, but in the safe zone it creates to meet others who share the same level of interest in the subject, and have the same reason to be there. In a conversation with another participant, we can either choose to stick to the script of just being there for the program (safe, no interaction), or explore further if we start to trust the other. Similarly, when a neutral and powerless organization invites powerful competitors, or clients and suppliers, or government bodies and companies, for a meeting on a shared subject—yes, the subject is officially of interest to them all, but it is also a safe zone with rules of conduct to allow people to learn more about each other.

Buffer zones are common, disguised under many names and pretexts. They are more neutral than institutions, we trust the social protocols they offer, letting us interact with strangers across business and cultural divides.

When we act in trusting ways, at any of these levels: personally, institutionally, or using buffer zones, we increase trust overall. Trust is complicated. It can be somewhat transferrable—people trusting me may also trust my friends to some extent. But it is not wholly so. It can be viral— upward spirals of trust occur when we trust and negative spirals occur when trust is broken. Trust can be highly specific—only this transaction or activity. And it can be vast—faith in a person, institution, or process. Trust can decay if it is not renewed through further activity. Acting with high levels of trust is a form of altruism that tends to be pragmatic. Trust, in all these ways, acts as a catalyst.

Social flows rely on trust between multiple layers, such as between individuals and institutions, processes, or buffer zones. Their cultivation requires deep attention to what lubricates appropriate trust.

Outperforming Hierarchy

Hierarchy was an innovation that helped humans transcend some of Dunbar's number limitations. We moved trust from a person to a structure and process. But it has limits too: information first needs to flow up and then down to the appropriate person or group.

A natural network easily outperforms a hierarchy in terms of efficiency and speed. A hierarchy seems very efficient at first glance. In a hierarchy the person at the top doesn't need to know the people at the bottom or even in the middle. Each person has a limited number of connections: this looks efficient and convenient...

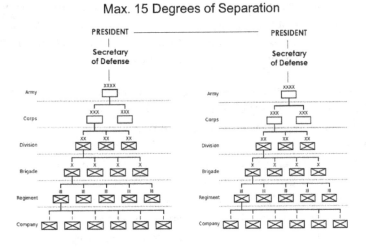

Figure 1. Functional hierarchy

... but it takes its toll. Take for instance two hierarchies each with 5 layers below the boss. If a strict hierarchy in communication were enforced, where all communication would only go to the top and back, it would require 11 handshakes to reach from the bottom of one hierarchy to the top, cross over and then move down to the lowest layer of the second hierarchy. And as we know from kindergarten, the message gets distorted after so many steps. Slow, tortuous, inefficient, and ineffective compared to a natural network where only a few (1, 2 or at most 3) handshakes would suffice to reach everyone.

No wonder everybody wants to (and does) bypass the hierarchy in practice, whenever convenient and possible. Still, for decision-making and coordination of large groups, hierarchy in various forms has been the standard methodology for transcending the social limits of our minds.

For identifying effective social flows, the real relationship network (an overlay on hierarchies) is very important. This is how new ideas get communicated, including new ideas on how we design our agreements and laws. While hierarchy is not antithetical to social flow, other network patterns tend to be more efficient and effective.

Social Technology

> Social technologies offer other means for overcoming the limits of our social brains. In _The Origin of Wealth_, Eric Beinhocker explores the origins of the seemingly infinite creation of wealth we are experiencing. One obvious factor is physical technology, our "mastery of nature," as the examples of Newton or Einstein and their contemporaries show. Another is how we, as a society, organize our combined efforts.

Cooperation requires time and energy. There is always the looming danger of abuse of trust and abuse of dependencies. But we need cooperation to generate more wealth through specialization.

According to anthropologists it is still possible to find small tribes of hunter-gatherers and farmers who do not specialize and where each extended family group, therefore, leads an autarkic life. This is usually a brutal and hard life: people living in very small, self-sufficient groups are usually threatened by disease and experience very little comfort. The rest of us, by contrast, have chosen to specialize and to cooperate in order to create wealth.

Autarkic:	quality of being self-sufficient

Specialization and cooperation means, in its simplest form, for example, that several people are involved in producing the same loaf of bread. Each person performs one step of the process, instead of one person performing all of the steps in sequence. A farmer grows wheat, the miller then produces flour from the wheat, and the baker bakes bread from the flour. At some point we discovered that specialization and cooperation produced much more, much better, and much more varied bread for the same effort as is required by autarkic production: in this way, we created wealth. For this arrangement to work, we had to invent some specific rules and conventions: how to trade the efforts and goods between the farmer, the miller, and the baker so that everyone was satisfied; how to balance the number of farmers, bakers, and millers; how to reward inventiveness in a way that increases productivity over laziness and free-ridership, and so on.

And, above all, we had to create a level of trust that gives everyone enough peace of mind that we can risk specialization. For specialization and cooperation come with a price: increased dependence on others. Dependence is scary in itself, and trust is the antidote you need to allow greater dependence. We have increased specialization to a fine art. The result is that we, as individuals, have gotten accustomed to products and services that we not only cannot produce ourselves, but would not even know how to produce. We are extremely dependent on many unknown and unseen others for even a simple piece of food packaged in plastic. Yet many of us trust that tomorrow there will be a new cheap supply of food that can be purchased, that water will flow from the tap, and electricity from the socket.

Money is based on trust as well. Money was one of the vital innovations supporting specialization. Money quantified the exchange, referenced it to a common standard and made the exchange storable, transferable in time and in location. You don't have to trust the individual as much if you can trust the money you get. But money is just worthless paper (or bits) if you do not trust that the token (paper, coins, or bits) will be accepted at face value by others.

Beinhocker places social technology as the counterpart to the physical technology needed to reap the benefits of specialization by inducing the right kinds of cooperation. Money is one such technology; government, law and the courts, property, corporations, schools, religion, hierarchy, marriage, rituals, and many others are manifestations of social technology. All of them are agreements between people on ideas, on concepts, on protocols.

Social technology is as important as physical technology in allowing society to function. As with physical technology, social technology is not static but evolving as we experiment and learn. In today's highly networked world we are starting to evolve more nuanced means of trust and exchange, with ideas like social capital and influence. These are enabling new forms of flow, larger networks, and even greater levels of specialization.

Man-Made, Man-Modifiable

The main difference between social technology and something like physics is that, for social technology, there are no fixed "laws of nature"—no experimentally verifiable models that guarantee a repeatable result given an input, no matter how hard some sciences like economics have tried to formulate "laws" in this sense. Complexity science and the network view of society have shown us the reason why.

Even a relatively small network (let alone a vast network of people) can exhibit a variety of behaviors that is computationally impossible to analyze completely. We have no mathematics yet to model and predict anything this complex, and brute force <u>computational methods fail quickly</u>.

Added to that are the emergent properties of the network. Emergent behavior is defined as the collective behavior of a network of actors that cannot be constructed from the rules governing the individual actors. You can analyze the rules, but it is nearly impossible to deduce, from these rules, the collective behavior that will emerge in a given instance. What will the swarm actually do today?

Take the famous example of ants searching for food: the observed collective behavior of a colony is fantastically rich and adaptive, yet simulations show that most likely an individual ant is following three very simple rules:

➢ Search at random to find food.

➢ When food is found, go back to the colony with food and leave a scented trail on the way back.

➢ When crossing a scented trail, follow that trail away from the colony.

It's the interaction between ants that elevates the collective behavior and exposes the emergent rich property. This is a flow produced by ants.

The ant example shows that relationships and the rules governing relationships matter in a network: a change in relationships and rules modifies the emergent properties of the network and thereby the health of the collective. The difference between us and ants is that we humans are aware of both the rules and the collective result. We actively try to influence the result. We consciously design and test the rules and interactions, by trial and error, as we observe our own emergent behavior. The famous "invisible hand" of Adam Smith, for example, is a description of an emergent property of the actions of many individuals interacting in trade. We may call it "free trade," but even free trade is governed by rules, protocols, and agreements.

It follows that if rules, protocols, and agreements are man-made, they also can be modified by man, leading to different results and different flows.

Biomimicry and Process Hierarchy

In the last few decades, engineers who design stuff have started to look more and more to nature for inspiration. It turns out that life has come up with elegant, efficient and beautiful solutions that we can try to replicate: this is called biomimicry. Innovations like Velcro come from imitating the way a burr attaches.

But biomimicry also has applications in social technology. To understand these, we need to look first at the enigma of life's origins. Terrence Deacon, in _Incomplete Nature_, shows how science is an extremely successful method for making sense of our world, but has, so far, failed to explain how life starts.

Physics, chemistry, biology, medical science, genetics, you name it: no hint of a theory that stands up to scrutiny. Deacon explores the existing theories, but they all end up eventually with a "homunculus" of one sort or another: you need life to start life. It's the chicken-and-egg question.

He picks a few defining characteristics of life to make his point:

➤ There is a boundary between the inside (cell, bacterium, virus, organ, animal, etc.) and the outside, which defines the remarkably stable entity you can observe.

➤ There is an exchange of energy and matter through the boundary (which scientists therefore call a "permeable membrane").

➤ The exchange of energy and matter is a necessary condition for the entity to stay alive.

➤ Some of the energy and matter is used to defend itself, repair damage, to grow and to replicate itself.

➤ All this is done by complex, biochemical interactions inside the entity, which even include the modification of complex molecules like DNA.

➤ There is some form of intent (at least in more sentient life forms than a one-celled life form).

The ongoing efforts of scientists have led to more and more understanding of parts of the mechanisms, parts of the biochemistry, parts of how genes work—but not to a theory that would explain how this could start from inanimate matter.

Biomimicry is useful for social technology because, when thinking about social flows, it also makes sense to think of your group or structure as a living entity with permeable membranes:

> There is a boundary which is permeable, through which information, energy and people flow both ways.

> You need energy and other resources to stay alive, mechanisms to defend, repair, grow and possible replicate it.

> Complex interactions are at work inside the group, using different skills and specialties, combined to fit for the task at hand, inventing new skills and processes on the go.

> There is an intent that guides the direction of growth and/or replication.

Complex living forms, like animals, show a process hierarchy. From the processes in a single cell, to organelles, to organs, to the animal itself. There are processes with flows that stay within the cell, but the membrane also permits flows between cells. These flows lead to the emergent behavior of the ensemble, which starts to act as an entity with another membrane that allows flows. Each level up, the same phenomenon is observed again and again. This is a process hierarchy.

Biomimicry enables us to look differently at group structures and the social technology that supports them. We can see entities (groups) with membranes (inside-outside) that support flows between the entities. Ensembles of entities emerge and these start to act together as an entity with a membrane. And so on.

For social flows, the benefit of the process hierarchy is that rather than having to submit to the egotistic whims of an authority figure in a functional hierarchy, we submit instead to a clear agreement and process which is transparent and collectively understood.

Given that our science cannot tell us how to design life, we are better off looking at our collective experience of dealing with living entities like plants and animals. That is called "cultivating."

Cultivating Social Flows

The word "design" triggers images of "Man Mastering Matter"; of the blood, sweat, and tears that go into developing a new car, a new cure, new software; of harnessing technology to create new powerful and beautiful tools.

Cultivating social flows is a different kind of design, intended to have an effect on society, on how we live and work and play together. New tools and new technology may play a crucial role in enabling new and better social flows but the cultivation effort is focused on the effect, how we enhance our lives as couples, friends, family, community, society.

Social Ecosystem:	a community of humans in conjunction with the living and nonliving components of their environment (things like air, water, and mineral soil), interacting as a system

The term "social flow" stresses the movement, the flow of energy, the constant evolution of the social ecosystem we call organizations and society. It is like life itself: you do not "design" life as a piece of technology, but you can influence and guide its development and evolution in ways that result in significant effects (both good and bad). We participate in social flows ourselves. Even more important, being part of a flow is an enormous help if you want to change it.

The Big Opportunity to Act Beyond Control

In a mechanical worldview someone or something is outside "the machine," is in control, therefore in a position to design and implement a change. If you are not in that position, you are "the machine" and you just follow orders.

That view explains the excuse "There is nothing I can do since I cannot control it (so I am not responsible)" or its corollary "I need to control and direct everything because I am responsible." This latter is a typical reaction from someone who recognizes that they can't control all the pieces involved and holds a Newtonian view of society as a machine.

Questions you can ask instead, however, include: Where do I have a choice to influence a flow? Where can I shift things, or create new options? What action is possible? Fortunately, there is a whole range of possible actions that go past black-and-white polarities: options that rely for their effect on guiding and influencing or nurturing.

The types of action that you can take and their range of intended outcomes can be matched with the three levels or spheres of influence in the Action Spectrum: control, guide, and nurture:

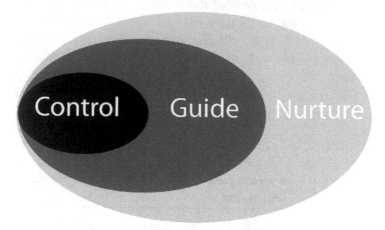

Figure 2. The spaces of the Action Spectrum

Figure 2 shows these levels as three ovals. The smallest oval is the limited area of what we can control. Moving outward, we can guide or influence in a wider range of situations. And finally, we can nurture in, or contribute to, the widest space.

The framing of the Action Spectrum always points to where you can act, through controlling, guiding, or nurturing. Depending on which layer of action you take, you can also determine what to expect or be certain about (and where there is uncertainty).

Actions on the Action Spectrum can be assessed in terms of:

➤ the possible types of relationships (from hierarchical, command-and-control relationships to dependent ones to relationships between equals)

➤ the time-scale before effects get visible (from immediate to years or even decades)

➤ the simplicity (or sophistication) of the model or metaphor (from designing a mechanical response to setting up complicated systems, up to designing for emergent behavior in complex systems)

➤ the metrics to evaluate with (from countable to milestone/ratable to outcome indicators)

(We will revisit how to use the Action Spectrum more specifically for evaluation in Part 4.)

The Action Spectrum model allows us to understand the work of many thinkers and practitioners. How do they choose their actions? What strategies do they use? Is there a natural sequence? How do they achieve traction, get the support needed, reach the collective desire to act and change within a group? What do case studies show about tactics we can use in practice?

It turns out there is an abundance of tools and practices available, for a wide variety of situations. Just one of these involves using expressions of gratitude in our personal relationships. These tools and interventions have network level impacts rather than just making transactional adjustments.

J *I have, for years now, had a personal practice around gratitude. It started with a simple five gratitudes a day challenge with a friend. Recently, when a friend contributed significant resources to a team project, I organized a gift from each team member to express different ways they were each appreciative of the lead contributor. Another member offered a vase to hold them. The generous contributor cried tears of joy while reading how she was seen and valued by the other team members. She can continue to go to the vase to read and be reminded of the powerful value she provided the team.*

We humans seem to thrive on a sense of fulfilled reciprocity. The gratitude vase helped the team absorb the generous gift of resources by giving back meaning and appreciation, creating a deeper sense of intimacy and connection within the team.

In another case, I publicly offered a total of 10 hours (1 hour each) for people to try my services. Danielle responded, "I would love to have an hour of your time, but I am not in a position to hire you right now. Is the offer okay for me to accept?" I confirmed it was not conditional on potential to hire. And so we agreed to a time. Toward the end of the conversation, I asked a question that triggered something useful for Danielle. Then the conversation ended. A month or two later, Danielle came back, sharing the story of how her life had changed dramatically since we had spoken. Of course none of the changes were because I created them, but still Danielle felt strongly that the shift she had made came from the conversation with me. Danielle offered to help on my book, giving

> *hours of editing time, making connections, and championing my work. I gifted one hour of high quality time, and Danielle returned many hours' worth because of gratitude she felt for what resulted (from her own efforts) as a consequence of the conversation. Gratitude can powerfully move people toward generosity and create more value.*

One example of the available tools and practices is technology that enables new social flows in traffic management.

Traffic management has been invented because we, as humans, are limited by what our senses tell us. As pedestrians, skaters, and cyclists in a park, we do not need traffic management to tell us how to move around safely in a crowded place, and any failures tend to be low-cost incidents that are mended quickly with an apology. Humans have a well-developed ability to sense how other people are moving, where objects are, and how to adapt our movements interactively. We use subtle signaling cues to show others our intentions. The flow of players on a basketball field, or couples on a crowded dance floor are living proof of that ability. Even driving in a car on crowded roads is built upon that ability: we have learned that adding some simple rules for behavior is all that is needed to get a relatively safe process. (And the struggle to automate that in self-driving cars shows how truly complex that task is). The interesting thing is that the "language" of the road by which we signal to each other differs from country to country. Driving in the USA and in Italy are two quite different experiences, let alone in countries like India.

In fast planes or trains or large ships, our senses are inadequate for the task: the speeds are too high or the reaction times (braking or steering) are too long, given the cost of errors. The solution has been to construct traffic management: an authority which controls and directs exactly what and how a plane or train can move, how fast, what direction, what corridor to follow.

It works, but only by severely limiting the options that are available.

The same can be said for traffic management of very busy roads in cities and suburbs: single drivers are unable to sense the total flow of cars and adapt to that flow so an authority takes over by installing crude limitations on what is possible. This is safe but wasteful if, for example, you end up waiting at a red traffic light, and nobody crosses the junction.

At some point demand will put pressure on the limitations: more sophistication will be needed and there will be a constant pressure to upgrade and enhance the traffic management to allow more options.

Increasing the heterogeneity of such integral management systems seems very hard, very costly and difficult to do, as practice shows.

Cultivating social flows means that you leave the management systems behind and turn back to that incredible ability we humans have for interacting movements. Why not try to enable that flow again, using technology to enhance our senses?

Can that be done? Yes: we are doing it, often without realizing it. In maritime traffic (seafaring ships) an Automatic Identification System or AIS has been introduced. An AIS system uses a radio transmitter on a ship that broadcasts for some 40-50 miles the current speed, the direction/plotted course and the characteristics/name of the vessel. Anyone with an AIS receiver within that range can pick up the signal and plot it on an interactive map on a monitor. The map shows where you are, what your heading and speed is, and what ships are around you. You see their speed and heading, and their characteristics: you see the large oil tanker and where it is heading, or any other ship in the vicinity. You can assess visually how your own course intersects with their paths, helped by software.

All modern ships have an AIS transceiver nowadays and use that information to communicate with each other. So when you are sailing a small ship across the busy English Channel in bad weather at night, you can "see" the other ships. The captains of the ships that are in each other's neighborhood can talk over the mariphone, communicating their intentions. Ok, we agree: "I, on the small ship, will reduce speed and change course to pass behind the big containership, no problem sir, you are welcome."

Technology enhances the senses of the captains, allowing for a social flow as if they were pedestrians in a park crossing each other's path. No need for a traffic management system. The AIS acts as an intervention that creates a network and enables new, socially mediated, flows.

In both cases, using gratitude as a tool and enabling social flows in traffic management, someone took it upon themselves to initiate a design to cultivate social flows, while being part of the subject at hand.

Key Concepts in this Chapter

How Social Flows Work

Networks
  - Flows Interactions as a Network

Trust
  - Dunbar's Number
  - Proxy
  - Self-Interest
  - Pay forward

Levels or Zones of Trust
  - Outperforming hierarchy

Social Technology
  - Agreements, forms, relationships, behaviors, laws, and concepts
    developed to create wealth through cooperation

Man-Made, Man-Modifiable

Biomimicry and Process Hierarchy

Cultivating Social Flows
  - Social Ecosystem

Act Beyond Control (Action Spectrum)
  - Control
  - Guide
  - Nurture

PART TWO:
REFRAMING AND NAVIGATING FOR SOCIAL FLOWS

CHAPTER 3:

REFRAMING

After interviewing and reading essays from practitioners, having numerous conversations and reflecting on our own practices, we have concluded that the first phase of cultivating social flows often begins with a reframe. In this chapter we explore what we mean by a reframe (or remapping) and we share some historical examples. We look at the conditions under which reframes arise and the conditions that contribute to a readiness for reframing. We look too at what makes a reframe coherent—what kinds of culture help it take shape and gain traction? Also we share the wisdom some practitioners have developed from their experience of working with reframing.

Breaking How It is Seen and Creating a New Way to See It

Models Are Not Reality

To begin our journey into cultivating social flows, we dig into the roots from which they grow and form: our stories about the world (and the models those stories suggest). Our minds rely on metaphors and models to make sense of our world, to filter the incredible amount of information we encounter into something we can handle. We use heuristics to make learning and decision-making manageable. We think both consciously and subconsciously in models, communicate in models, and sometime delude ourselves by thinking that the model is all there is.

The conscious act of trying to understand the world through hypothesis and mathematical modeling, and verifying those models and hypotheses with experiments, has given us a fabulous grip on nature. We modeled how atoms form molecules. We modeled how energy and light behave. We modeled how photosynthesis works.

Working with models tends to be a learning experience over time. We like to think our models are accurate or even fixed truths, but most, if not all, models are only prototypes.

One of the co-founders of **London Creative Labs** (LCL), for instance, had studied the work of microfinance legend Muhammad Yunus. Over many years LCL built up models of how social change could happen in communities. And locally, they had a model designed to help them understand the social issues in Brixton, South London. They believed that helping give people the skills and connections to become entrepreneurs would be a game-changer for the community. So the founders, **Sofia Bustamante** and **Mamading Ceesay**, built a program to provide entrepreneurship training.

Only it didn't work as well as they hoped. Turns out that before you can use the skills to start even a small company, you have to believe in yourself and your value. So, like any good entrepreneurs realizing the market didn't match their expectations, the founders reworked their offering. They started a program to teach coaching. What they discovered is that people could clear their resistance to believing in themselves through both the content of the coaching as well as through basic belief adjustment: "You can't help your peer if you have nothing to give. You can see you are helping your peer. Thus, you must have something to give." LCL learned through experience that a person's ability to change their circumstances is deeply entrenched in what they believe their relationship to the world is. They write as follows in their essay on CultivatingFlows.com about the tribal leadership model developed by Dave Logan and John King which they used (along with a similar Aikido framework):

The Tribal Leadership model

Mindset: the overarching narrative of the person's inner dialogue.

Level 1: the world is dangerous. It's fucked. I have to fight to survive.

Level 2: the world can be great for others. But not for me.

Level 3: the world can be great for me. But I must hide my weaknesses and it's a competitive world. I'm on my own. Somehow, no one is ready, willing or able to help me, so I can only rely on myself.

Level 4: the world can be great for us—for our organization/team/ community. Let's not get stuck in my or your individual agenda. There's no I in team. It's all about We not Me, the sum is greater than the parts and we can all get our needs met by working together. (Zappos)

Level 5: the world can be great for everyone (Nelson Mandela, Buckminster Fuller)

Assessing which level people function from can help customize the support they need to shift into entrepreneurship.

The tribal leadership model explains worldviews, demonstrating that the theories we develop about how the world works may be quite different from how it actually works or how other people think it works. Beliefs, models, and worldviews form a spectrum of our story-telling about how the world is and how it works.

But it is so tempting to assume that the model is all there is, that reality has no other factors. If it is not in the model, can it be understood within the model, or is it even visible to users of the model? If not, does it really exist? We are all familiar with the series of changes we as a collective have gone through as we modeled how the solar system works. Now, it seems surprising that at one time we thought it all revolved around us.

History shows a long succession of such breakthroughs, where the dominant idea, ideology or scientific theory turned out to be incomplete, incorrect, or just plain wrong, and we replaced it with a better, more seemingly accurate version.

Models and metaphors are great tools, but beware of mistaking the map for the territory; the model for the world. That is in many cases not even a conscious mistake. Our minds subconsciously extrapolate conclusions within a fraction of a second, based on limited, and usually insufficient, data. We act upon them, often without much consideration. We become habituated to the models we use until we forget they are models of the world and slip into believing that is how the world works.

Daniel Kahneman collects a vast amount of data from thousands of experiments in his book _Thinking, Fast and Slow_, revealing how our conscious, "rational" mind is influenced by these conclusions: for instance, in the way that we assess risks. The same heuristic shortcut that helps us act very fast under pressure can be a weakness when we "see" patterns and models that may not be there at all, jumping to the wrong conclusions. Magicians, con artists, and spin doctors exploit that tendency for misdirection in everyday life, and the consequences of those weaknesses can be less than entertaining.

Influence

The power of models and metaphors or even words is amazing. The stories people have, the words that they use, inform the actions they take and think are possible. If we have a word for something, it means we have a mental model for it, and a token (word) that we can use to communicate about it, think about it, imagine or dream about it. We can package up whole ideas into word or image memes that travel like a thought or belief virus.

Meme:	a cultural analogue to a gene, conveying an idea

The opposite is true as well: not having words or models or metaphors restricts what we can conceive, limiting us in what we can imagine. Everybody knows the feeling of searching for the right word, a new word, to express what we want, and not finding it. Or trying to find the right translation of a word from another language. It is a fact that it's easier to discuss, for instance, philosophy in some languages than others, because there are more words and associated models available. Words can become the keys to new possibilities.

Memes can operate like core belief viruses, permeating our cultures. Memes, like genes, are the carriers that the life of ideas rests on. We spoke with a meme scientist, **Balázs László Karafiáth** tracking the flow and association of words around climate change. He told us:

We gathered more than 5,000 climatememes, pieces of thoughts from conversation, tweets, Facebook posts that contained "climate change" or "global warming." We coded them for semantic content, and statistically analyzed them to reveal the underlying structure of the discourse around climate change. In this exercise we wanted to dig deep and unveil the underlying meme structures when we think about climate change or global warming.

In our research on climate memes each of the 5,000 memes we gathered from Twitter was retweeted at least once and stands on its own as a unique thought or behavior that has been successfully shared by at least two people. By mapping out the correlations across different memes, we were able to reveal the resonance points that define the underlying psychology of the global warming conversation. These resonance points all have what we call "meme dimensions" in our report and there are five of them: Harmony, Survival, Cooperation, Momentum, and Elitism.

The global warming meme is this web of cultural expressions about the human relationship with nature (Harmony), with one another (Cooperation), and the threat of extinction for the human race (Survival) that evokes a wide diversity of sentiments about expert

authority and political power (Elitism). This is what appears in the
data when it is analyzed for memetic structure.

After sharing the psychological threads of these five expressions, Karafiáth writes, "The culture as an ecosystem does not react well to the climatememe so far. It is psychologically toxic to the human mind and won't spread outside a small group." He talks about it in biological terms, as if resisting the climate change conversation was an immune response within the collective body. It is clearly in need of a reframe—a new meme—that can overcome the immune response from the collective.

Human social systems have immune system-like reactions to these idea viruses. No matter how well-engineered or well-intentioned a meme might be, it has to survive the immune system response. This is similar to the process <u>Thomas Kuhn</u> describes in <u>*The Structure of Scientific Revolutions*</u> where new ideas are at first resisted until they eventually become a compelling explanation for phenomena that can't be explained with the current model. Some memes may seem innocuous, like cat videos on the Internet, but others shape the structure of what we believe is possible, and the stories we tell about ourselves and the world.

The act of reframing is a creative one, inviting others to a new meme, model, or narrative.

Breaking the Limits

So, models and memes can be helpful. We create new ones to overcome old ones we have become stuck in. When we discover a limit or barrier in a model, we can change it. Being aware of the models and heuristics helps. Then we can "think slow" when we need to.

Reframing the territory relies on introducing an alternative metaphor, a richer model, or a different emphasis. A new word, phrase, or idea opens up the possibility for people to dream up actions and imagine paths they could not see before. Words and models allow the new idea to be communicated, to be discussed, to be enriched, to become the start for new social flows.

The words may be simple.

Take, for example, the words "markets" and "consumers." Markets and consumers are technical terms in the science of economics with a specific meaning in that context. They have however become household expressions, used on the news, in talk-shows, by politicians. The drawback of these household terms is that we are painted as passive actors driven by laws of nature bigger than us: we are anonymous "consumers" who buy stuff in "markets" and make choices to consume according to the laws of economics. It can make you feel small and insignificant, subordinate to a greater god with an invisible hand.

The expression "we are the economy" is a reframe: it changes the perspective. This phrase is all about you and me, living our lives, trying to make a better future for ourselves, friends, family, and children or grandchildren. The division of labor, institutions, and companies into what we call markets is nothing more or less than a man-made design to fulfill that desire. In this perspective we are empowered: every time you buy something you vote for the kind of future you want. You vote for what institution/company gets a better chance for survival. Even bolder: if the design of the markets does not deliver the goods or otherwise does not meet our goals, then we can change the design. All the institutions and companies and rules are there to support us, not the other way around.

Reframing can be highly disruptive, for better or worse. Reframing can turn perception upside down in powerful ways, allowing for new flows, opening up possibilities never dreamt of. As with most ideas, reframing is a tool that also can be used for devious purposes: a trick used by the newest C-level executive or manager to try to rewire the company, leaving their fingerprint and legacy behind them, if their ego comes before organizational thriving. Or a tool that manipulators or spin doctors use to hide uncomfortable truths.

Why is an Idea Hot?

There is an abundance of ideas floating around in any given moment. Every day more and more are being generated, blogged, tweeted, or talked about. Most of them wither in silence, are forgotten the next day, and do not get traction. But some *do* get picked up, build in strength, and do not go away even when the idea and its proponents are violently opposed. You could even say that the violence of the opposition is proportional to its staying power. What makes the difference between the ones without effect and the ones that stay?

When Thomas Piketty published his book, _Capital in the Twenty-First Century_, he probably did not expect to be lauded and despised worldwide, to become the topic of hot debates between people who probably had not even read his book and knew little of economics, and to be received as a rockstar of economics. He did introduce an extremely successful reframe, which we would summarize as: *income and capital inequality is an inbuilt propensity of the design of capitalism; it has risen again over recent decades to previously unseen levels and that is a bad thing that needs to be corrected.*

It is radically different from the idea that *inequality is a natural result of differences between people, and a necessary stimulant to create progress.* And his idea suddenly became central to many debates.

The point we are trying to make is not about his ideas being right or wrong. What is interesting is why this reframe had so much power, even when it was an "accidental" reframe resulting from a professional investigation. After all, he is not the first to have said something like this during the last couple of decades.

What helped is that he backed up his claim with a massive amount of data, meticulously collected and correlated, unlike anything done before. By and large, nobody was able to dent that foundation of data, and not for lack of trying, by the way.

In our view the clinching factor was the unrest that has been brewing in society in recent years about income and capital. Something didn't feel right, especially the story that the rich deserve their wealth, and everybody else will benefit from it eventually. For more and more people, that was simply not how they experienced things.

Capital in the Twenty-First Century gave a solid foundation for that feeling, catalyzed individual discontent into a collective voice, fronted by opinion leaders. The result is that inequality is on the agenda and has become a topic to have an opinion about, to study, to make policies for.

A less successful part of the reframe has been Piketty's recommendations in the second part of his book. They are nowhere to be seen in discussions.

What we noticed from this example:

➢ It was not the originator of the idea but other people, especially multiple opinion leaders with a voice, who gave the reframe its power. They took the idea and backed it up, supporting it with their reputation which tapped into pent-up flows. Ideas don't move without first having followers.

➢ The time was right. A lot of people were waiting for a trigger.

➢ The reframe gave people hope, initiated the development of a narrative that showed a path to a better life, an improved situation. The latent energy was transformed into actionable stories, things you could discuss with others, so that you did not feel alone in your desire, so that you could feel vindicated.

> The reframe was thoroughly founded in facts and data, strong enough to win over skeptics with an open mind, strong enough to get open support against opposition.

> Reframing is the necessary start of a journey, but it's not enough on its own. To get results you need more—you need the next steps—as we explore in the coming chapters.

Historic Reframes

The study of history becomes even more interesting when we start to look for evidence of successful reframes. We've already mentioned the moment when discoveries were made that overturned the idea that the sun revolved around the earth. Other big moments occurred when social technology reframes, which we now find obvious, happened. These reframes take the form of a reconstruction that involves working back from the scaled implementation to the core idea that had to be adopted as something new and unknown but worth pursuing.

Take the example of the birth of accounting, taxation and writing. It is generally agreed that writing was invented in Mesopotamia around 4,000 BCE (and later, independently, in China and Mesoamerica). Denise Schmandt-Besserat describes in her book, _How Writing Came About_, how a series of social technology inventions paved the way for writing to emerge.

Around 8,000 BCE, humanity started to use clay tokens. Small objects of many shapes—like cones, cylinders, spheres, and disks—served as counters.

The idea of using tokens evolved to meet the needs of a society that went beyond subsistence to a form of wealth and specialization. It became necessary to count, and to store that count in something less ephemeral and error-prone than memory of speech. Clay tokens became the agreed protocol for storing counts—a simple thing in our eyes, which must have been a major conceptual leap for the Mesopotamians. What yesterday was a piece of clay became today the evidence of the size of your grain reserves. Tokens were used first to count the products of farming and later to count goods manufactured in workshops (though, according to Schmandt-Besserat there is no evidence of tokens being used in trade. Tokens were tools of the state.)

Wealth and specialization paved the way for the development of the "rank society," where some are "more equal than others." Taxation and redistribution, backed up by the monopoly of power, relied on volumes produced being counted and accounted for—and the taxes you could levy on these volumes. This was something made possible by tokens.

With this plethora of tokens, the accountants needed a way to store tokens in archives. One of the popular archives was a simple hollow clay ball in which the tokens were placed. The clay balls would be sealed with fresh clay to prevent theft and fraud. We can guess that sealing the pot you could not then see how many tokens were inside. The solution was to imprint the shapes of the tokens in the fresh clay surface. The number of units was expressed by repeating the imprint: a clay ball holding seven spheres would bear seven impressions of spheres on the outside.

Reframe: the imprint of a token represents the same as the token itself.

At some point, possibly thousands of years later, the next leap was taken. You could just as well count and keep track using just the imprints: Why bother with invisible tokens in a clay ball? Just take a fresh clay tablet and imprint that with tokens. And if you could do that, you could also use a pointed stylus to add signs to the impressions, giving you a richer and more legible set of pictographs. A clay tablet can be transported, as a proof and a means of communicating.

Reframe (along with another abstraction): a tablet can be portable evidence of that which it represents—the step to cuneiform writing from that point on is easy to imagine.

The power of reframing—each step leading to another in an evolutionary path—is visible in this story. To recap:

> A token in the form of a sphere is not a sphere as such at face value, but an abstract item replacing the physical item you want to keep track of: a token as representation of the real thing. A revolutionary thought at that point in time.

> The next step up is: an imprint is not just an imprint. It is the equivalent of the token. Another big step, that led to the thought that the imprint is just as good as the token as a way to represent the physical object.

> You could make a new type of imprint other than by pressing a model in clay, which allowed for a much richer set of code.

We take this for granted nowadays, yet looking back, these steps must have been a revolution for the people of that time. They certainly reshaped their society as information became storable and transferable, accountable to those in power.

The lack of records of this period in history forces us to make assumptions about how this reframing came about, and how it took hold, got operationalized and accepted as the new standard. All we can see is the end result. Most likely the desire to be able to count and have a reliable memory of that count fueled the first adaption of tokens. Once they were widely available, few rulers could fail to see the opportunity presented by these ideas; accounting and taxation are basic tools for anyone in power, so they would most likely support the adoption.

The take-away is that when looking at history, and at historical reframes that created change, one should search for the "energy" that drove adoption of the ideas. There is always resistance to change, therefore a reframe has to tap into a source of willpower, of reasons why people want to take on this new venture. In Piketty's case it was discontent; in Mesopotamia, it was, most likely, the opportunity created by wealth and specialization.

Triggers to Reframe

In these examples, you can see that to consciously reframe something is a creative act. The reframe needs to get adoption, and needs to trigger a source of motivation and energy for people. To accept change, to go for the opportunity, and to keep on going even if there are setbacks, takes courage and determination. While they may seem to act magically once adopted, the creation and growth of a reframe are rarely simple.

In our research, we have not found a single or simple recipe for reframing. It is a piece of the art of cultivating social flows. Much has happened by accident of circumstance. Somewhat less happens intentionally.

We can, like trendwatchers, attempt to spot a reframe emerging in the zeitgeist. We can look locally or globally to see where attention is shifting from an old version to a new meme or model. Take Basic Income, for example. The meme is already in motion. The idea is decades old with a wide range of advocates, but now it is gaining traction. Somehow it is catching a rising energy, showing up in experiments on multiple continents. It is even part of a Y Combinator research project. It seems to be gaining momentum, especially in light of a story emerging about how robots will take most jobs. If people do not need to work in order for us to have our needs met, what might an economy look like? Basic income might be one way to answer that.

But as well as grabbing a wild reframing that's already in progress, we can instead focus on intentionally shifting the way others perceive the world by creating a new reframe. To do so requires immersion, sensing the flow as it is, beyond the accepted wisdom. It is like getting in the mud with an alien anthropologist's curiosity.

To find flows in need of reframing and sense their ripeness for change, we see some patterns in creativity. It helps, for example, to identify the assumptions that are not discussed any more by anyone, that are treated as dogmas that are not questioned, ones that limit what can be discussed. These so-called "sacred cows" can point to opportunities to innovate. Reframing may be based on overturning one of the core dogmas or assumptions, and there is nothing more powerful than that, if the reframe is accepted. Or seeing an Einsteinian insanity: doing the same thing over and over again and expecting different results. Or hearing about dilemmas, where two different worldviews co-exist that contradict each other. If there is frustration in a flow linked to any of these, there is some energy available for a reframe.

To find opportunities for reframing we can look at where current frames experience unrest or have some tension with new data or evidence. Then we use the new data to develop a better frame to describe the phenomenon. **Jon Husband** writes about Wirearchy in the essay he contributed to our project. Husband's work on Wirearchy captures the shift from top-down organizational structures to networks of activity. Knowledge was power and bred hierarchy in the past. Now structure is seen as a barrier to the free flow of knowledge (and power), while Wirearchy enables the sharing of knowledge as needed. This single word, as the carrier of an idea, is a powerful call to a new way to think about, and shape, organizations. It acknowledges the frustration most of us have with hierarchy while describing a new option for solving the challenge of knowledge flows.

We found that there are four key indicators that the situation is primed for a reframe. The necessary energy can be derived from unspoken unrest, frustration, and tension:

➢ *Stuckness*: the dominant idea does not work any more as expected; everyone feels it but there is no alternative (or so it seems).

➢ *Saturation*: the market is saturated and growth is not possible.

> ➤ _Aversion_: the focus is purely on what's wrong with the current situation.

> ➤ _Air sandwiches_: there is a wider and wider gap between "official" statements and the reality people perceive.

Stuckness

This often arises in science, leading to what Thomas Kuhn labelled "Paradigm Shifts" where an idea comes along that explains what the existing idea has failed to explain. Newtonian physics only got us so far. It dealt well with problems on a human scale. Einstein's work helped explain phenomena on a different scale where Newtonian physics fell short. Stuckness also arises in politics, governance strategies, and business.

For example, offshoring helped businesses move to cheaper labor sources overseas, which became a dominant idea in business practice. Yet growing unemployment domestically has led to public outrage as a response to it. Companies are stuck between needing to reduce costs and improve public perception of their brands. _The Economist_ reported in January 2013 that: "High levels of unemployment in Western countries after the 2007-2008 financial crisis have made the public in many countries so hostile towards offshoring that many companies are now reluctant to engage in it." Some have suggested "reshoring" as a reframe, claiming reduced shipping cost as an advantage.

Look for opportunities to reframe a stuck situation by examining the seemingly unquestionable elements of it.

Saturation

Innovation Saturation happens with markets that are fully penetrated. Thomas Osenton, author of _The Death of Demand_, says, "Every product or service has a natural consumption level. We just don't know what it is until we launch it, distribute it, and promote it for a generation's time (20 years or more) after which further investment to expand the universe beyond normal limits can be a futile exercise." For example, there is a limit to how many cups of coffee a person can drink in one day, and to the number of people willing to drink coffee—we can determine a maximum amount of coffee that could be consumed per day. And a new machine for making the coffee, grinding it, delivering it, serving it, is also going to have limits of market penetration. About the same time as Osenton was putting out his research on market saturation, <u>W. Chan Kim and Renée Mauborgne</u> put out *Blue Ocean Strategy*. Red oceans are, metaphorically, highly competitive, price optimized, lowering return markets. All blue ocean strategies are reframes. Cirque du Soleil offers an excellent example of a reframe and blue ocean strategy. Only so many people go to the circus and have for ages. There was not a lot of room for more circus, but by creating something that was half circus and half theater experience, Cirque du Soleil could draw from both of those markets (and other forms of entertainment) while charging a premium price.

Look for opportunities to reframe a saturated market or innovation space by considering the <u>adjacent possible</u>. To make this simple, go up a layer (for example, with Cirque du Soleil, up a layer from circus to "live entertainment") and then look at all the other areas within that group (other live entertainment: theater, comedy, opera, etc.) to see how any of them might be combined with what you have into something new.

Adjacent possible:	connecting or blending options within a parent category to create a viable new option

Aversion

This describes a situation where we have ideas about how to move away from how things are (which we don't want) but little sense of what we do, actively want. Sustainability, for example, focuses primarily on what we don't want, asking us to find a path away from a damaging and destructive present in order just to survive. On the other hand, the thrivability reframe transcends while it also includes sustainability. Thrivability focuses on what to move toward, expanding the story of possibility—going beyond the sustainable perspective of just surviving to a vision of a thriving world where people prosper and life flourishes. Just changing the story expands people's sense of what might be possible and gets the creative juices flowing with imagination.

Thrivability is an example of a reframe that moves us from "aversion" models towards "desire" models. "Aversion" models arise when we get clear about what we do not want to be, what is considered broken in the existing story. "Desire" models arise when we get clear about what direction we *do* actively want to go in.

Look for opportunities to flip from stagnating in aversion. It needn't just be about doing less of a "bad thing" but can instead be about doing more of the "right thing."

Air Sandwiches

In _The New How_, Nilofer Merchant's first book, she explains an air sandwich as the gap between what management says and what people are really doing. Here too is an opportunity for a reframe. People can function in spaces where there is a lack of alignment between talk and action, but the energy available for solving challenges will tend to be low or be used indirectly, via politics and positional power. When a group is out of alignment, with a gap between what they say and what they do, a new story can be introduced to increase integrity.

Look for opportunities to reframe air sandwiches by identifying where people feel out of integrity, where actions do not align with stories, or where products do not align with marketing. Consider what the return might be if you can approach the gap with a new solution and what story might galvanize enough support for that shift to take place.

These, then are four key approaches for generating a reframe. Either you have sensed a reframe emerging in the world or you have come up with an idea to offer. You want to start inviting a small inner circle to test it out and collectively build together, or you already have a team to work with. Here are some elements to consider in polishing that gem of an idea into something to make public.

Coherence for Reframing

It is the desire, motivation, and energy of people that fuels the flow of the new reframe. People have to want to participate and own it. People need to want to bring it further, if it is to succeed. And we are not as rational as we would like to believe ourselves to be. Whatever we want to tell ourselves, we don't obviously find the best solution and then actually implement it. We have egos, blind spots, cultural differences and personalities that influence the choices we make. We have different motives, different desires. There has to be some force that keeps these divergent energies together, to keep coherence.

The coherence is first of all brought about by the narrative, the story you tell each other about the purpose, its foundations, and about the road ahead. As you begin to test out a reframe, look at how it invites a narrative, how it guides behavior, and what it motivates in others.

Narratives

If I say "love triangle" then you immediately have a sense of what roles the characters are going to play, whatever their name and situation. If I say "epic adventure" then too you have a sense of roles that might be played because we all have a deep archive of the archetypes that are alive in these kinds of narratives. A rich narrative has many roles to choose from, which enable contributions from a wide variety of actors. Each "actor" uses the narrative to gain autonomy while contributing: ideally, it makes it possible for you to choose the task that fits your desire for mastery while contributing to the shared purpose.

The narrative allows a large diversity of people to contribute to the whole—the "we"—while satisfying their own motivation—their "me." Opportunity-based narratives invite participation and open up a sense of possibility. They are defined by the opportunities they create. They tend to be desire or "toward" narratives, rather than aversion or "away from" narratives.

Aversion narratives tend to be less generative, focusing on what to avoid instead of where to go together. Aversion narratives trigger our disgust and encourage us to be indignant, angry, and resistant. Opportunity-based narratives capture our imagination and encourage us to wonder.

You see two people cutting rocks. Suppose you ask the first what he is doing, and he replies, "cutting rocks," but when you ask the second, he replies, "building a cathedral." The second has enrolled in an opportunity-based narrative.

John Hagel, co-author of _The Power of Pull_, distinguishes between stories and narratives: "stories are self-contained (they have a beginning, middle and resolution) and they're about the storyteller or some other people, they're not about the listener. In contrast, narratives are open-ended, they are yet to be resolved, and their resolution depends upon the choices and actions of the listener. As a result, they're a powerful call to action, emphasizing the ability that we all have to make a difference." Stories are often in the first person. Narratives are in the second person—the agent in the story is you, the reader or audience. Narratives call us into action and their outcomes are determined by the actions we take. They are participative.

Narratives, according to John Hagel, "are also a powerful way to address the cognitive biases that grip us in times of high uncertainty and rapid change." In other words, narratives are essential for reframing.

It cannot be stressed enough: a good narrative is open-ended, yet to be resolved, and the resolution depends upon the choices and actions of the listener. The listener should become a participant, start owning the development of the narrative together with other listeners, contribute to its growth, and spread the word.

A narrative is carried by people, exchanging and enhancing it in a structure or shape, and using protocols to decide what to add. All this may be implicit at this stage of development. In reframing, open-endedness of the new narrative is of the utmost importance, especially when dealing with a core group that carries the existing story. Quite often a specific field or interest has a small group of people who everybody turns to (eventually) on a particular subject for information, know-how and "know-why," and history. Hubs like this can be found even in big corporations or bureaucratic institutions, quite often not in positions of bureaucratic power. In many cases they form an invisible network, sharing knowledge and bypassing formal channels.

They are the first ones to notice if there is a need for reframing, even if they do not articulate it as such. Stagnation, frustration over lack of progress, a widening gap between reality as they experience it and the official story, strategy decisions that they perceive as catastrophic—all these create a sense of urgency.

If they adopt a new narrative arising from the reframing, because it gives them hope, this hub will be a strong foundation for the next step. When these people buy in, the question they will ask is about how to get things moving.

There is no need for a full consensus around the narrative. Don't waste energy on pulling in the stragglers; rather let people who buy-in self-select. Let them use their network of trust to find other supporters.

The development of the narrative in this phase requires secrecy, or at least not to be done in the limelight. Honing and refining the narrative, testing it against doubts and criticisms, searching for the dirty details, is best done in a safe environment. As the idea's network expands, the narrative may evolve.

Lessons from Experience

Go with the Flow

Trying to force the reframe to a plan is usually counterproductive: going with the flow is the right state of mind.

Reframes may already be in motion, and we simply catch them as we can. Reframes can take decades. We can take a leap of faith or we can join with our allies in a co-creative process. Because the size and scope of reframes varies so greatly, as do their triggers, there is no simple recipe for how long it takes to develop it before the next phase begins. Immersing yourself allows you to sense the opportunities and act upon them.

Whatever path brings you to reframe, it will be filled with uncertainty. We offer this book to give a general sense of the landscape of cultivating social flows, however every journey through that landscape will have much that is hard to predict. For some people this is thrilling, for others it is terrifying.

Yet the essence of reframing is a discovery of the unknown. Emergence of new and exciting ideas in the complexity of humanity relies on our ability to explore and live the not-yet-known. As Rainer Maria Rilke suggests:

> *Be patient toward all that is unsolved in your heart and try to love the questions themselves, like locked rooms and like books that are now written in a very foreign tongue. Do not now seek the answers, which cannot be given you because you would not be able to live them. And the point is, to live everything. Live the questions now. Perhaps you will then gradually, without noticing it, live along some distant day into the answer.*

Stairstep Exposure

Releasing a new reframe to a new wider audience is more than just repeating the narrative. In many stories we heard from practitioners they described a stairstep pattern: once you try to cross a threshold in size of the audience, a step had to be made. And there were more steps, more thresholds than one as the size of the exposure continued to grow. It did not feel like a continuum but more like stepchanges.

They described a step as going back and enhancing the narrative: how to embed the narrative in more context, how to adapt to new counterarguments and opposition, how to add more background information, how to add authority and attach social capital to balance the initial hesitation and reservations people have.

The reason for this is that, as the audience grows, two effects amplify each other:

> The first people attracted to the reframe probably already have invested a lot of time and energy in trying to find a new path, a new narrative. They are prepared and receptive, much more so than the second or third ring who need to take a bigger leap of faith.

> As the scale of the group grows, less interaction time is available for seeing how the narrative has started and evolved, to get to a point where someone understands the reframe and feels part of it.

The best practice is to pre-empt these effects. Once a reframe feels stable and accepted (in a certain size of group), play your own devil's advocate game: collect the "yes but…" questions, the often unspoken assumptions you have encountered. Secondly seek out friendly critics, test the reframe and the narrative on them, ask them for the same devil's advocate counterarguments, on what they expect the first defensive reaction will be. Thirdly, test and test again.

There are apparent exceptions to the stairstep exposure pattern. For example, Apple has the social capital to rapidly scale a reframe of what a phone or computer is or could be, because it is a trusted brand. The brand went through the stairstep process so the product rapidly follows the brand. The exceptions rely on the authority of the person or organization launching them (which is moving through the adoption cycle already).

Ethics, or How to Detect Abuse

As powerful as it is, there is the danger of misuse or even abuse of the potency of reframing. Power-hungry people may want to disrupt current productivity to make their mark, to challenge existing beliefs and culture, or just to show their dominance. Manipulators may inject insidious memes to further their interests.

Detecting the difference between benign and harmful remapping requires sensing the morality of the intent, of the energy that is tapped by the framing, of the timing of the new framing. Positive intent can be detected by signs like:

> ➢ In a situation of innovation saturation on the existing "map" or reality, there is unrest and tension. You can almost touch the craving for something better.

> ➢ The alternative opens up, gives hope and new energy, new even unknown possibilities.

> ➢ It lifts all boats.

Insidious intent can be detected by signs like:

> ➢ The reframe builds on fear and danger, on potential losses.

> ➢ It creates divisions and conflicts, choices between "us" and "them," "for" or "against."

> ➢ It creates unrest where there was none before.

One antidote to harmful reframing is widespread truthfulness, consistent fact-checking and testing of arguments, positions, and proposed evidence, supported by persons of reputation. This is hard work for a single person, but fast and effective if done by a network of people who have know-how and access to communication resources.

Reframing: Conclusion

Reframing or remapping the territory can powerfully influence the possibility space. We can create new memes that are symbols anchoring the new space, even create new ways of organizing with a different perspective. New connections, agreements, products, and services may arise in that space.

The coherence for reframing is first of all brought about by the narrative, the story you tell each other about the purpose, about the road ahead, about the foundation of the purpose. A rich narrative has many roles to choose from—this enables a wide variety of actors to contribute. Acknowledgment provides context for a reframe and may lead to additional advocacy and support. Gratitude and recognition is a powerful social reward for each person's contribution.

Reframing is a powerful tool. Shepherding the reframing and the power it unleashes requires care about coherence of the idea and the parties working together on it. As powerful as reframing is, there is the danger of the misuse or even abuse of its potency. Manipulators may inject insidious memes to further their interests. Protecting coherence means making sure that the power that is unleashed isn't co-opted.

It is wise to remember that reframing replaces or expands one set of models and metaphors with another. The new set of models lets us see different possibilities and thus the opportunity to create new flows. However, the new models are still models. They are incomplete and not necessarily more accurate, or even more durable. The new models simply provide greater utility for the moment. Hold them lightly too.

What about you? What have you found works in reframing? While we have pointed toward four of the ways that reframing can be done, there might be others. What have you discovered triggers a disruption in a current frame or meme? We will continue exploring this on the website where our collective knowledge can grow together. Stop in and share your wisdom and practice at CultivatingFlows.com.

Quick Guide to Reframing

Reframing relies on introducing an alternative metaphor, a richer model, or a different emphasis which opens up the possibility for people to dream up actions and paths they could not see before.

Breaking How It is Seen

➢ Our models or frames powerfully shape our sense of possibility.

➢ Reframing is potent and can have large, cascading impacts.

➢ A strong meme moves quickly beyond the control of its creator(s).

Why is an Idea Hot?

While there can't be an exhaustive list, we found a few characteristics that we think help make an idea hot:

➢ People are primed for it: they have the knowledge and beliefs in place to make the leap to it.

➢ Timing: the idea has ripeness within a larger context.

➢ It's rigorous and grounded in facts, which help give the idea staying power in the face of resistance.

➢ It's highly useful or answers a need that people have.

Triggers to Reframe

Several triggers may suggest an area is ready for reframing:

➢ Stuckness: the old model isn't working or doesn't apply to new situations.

➢ Saturation: the market is saturated and needs to be approached differently, such as blue ocean approach.

➢ Aversion: the current model says what not to do and there is opportunity to say what to move towards instead.

➢ Air sandwiches: there is a gap between what is being proclaimed and what is being implemented.

Hacking a Reframe

> ➢ Be creative, look for edge views.

> ➢ Explore tension and unrest in the current frame.

> ➢ Wonder about alternative possibilities, look for a switch from "away from" to a "towards" position.

> ➢ Seek siblings of the idea for new combinations.

> ➢ Recombine related ideas.

Coherence of Reframing

Narrative:

> ➢ Create compelling and inviting opportunity-based narrative.

> ➢ Seek out an implicit leadership hub, which may be hungry for a new story of possibility.

> ➢ Work through the narrative in a safe, secure circle before launching more broadly.

Warnings

> ➢ Go with the flow.

> ➢ Mind the stairsteps of adoption.

> ➢ Beware of the use of fear and division.

CHAPTER 4:

NAVIGATING

It is very satisfying to observe that a new reframe you have helped to develop triggers a positive response and attracts more people to the vision. As a reframe begins to take shape, what needs to happen before it can ripple through a social ecosystem? The pressure to convert the enthusiasm to action mounts: you and others feel this is the right thing to do and affirm each other in this belief. Yet in between reframing the new idea and operationalizing it, there lies a necessary step. Experience teaches us to go slowly in this phase in order to go longer and faster later. Mistakes we discover in our mental prototype are cheaper and easier to resolve than ones we find after we operationalize. Also, imaging together helps us clarify that we want the same things together, preventing hurt feelings and frustration down the line. In the Navigating phase, we want to scope out the landscape created by the new framing, test out some scenarios, and do some initial risk assessments.

We must go deeper, wider, and further, in the exploration of the reframe and its consequences, and we must do so with more and more people, resulting in more knowledge on how to navigate in this new world.

Navigating consists of exploring the new space and developing the best approach for how to achieve the dream. In the Navigating phase:

> ➢ Expand the community that explores, as diversity allows you to reach areas you cannot discover alone.

> ➢ Gather intelligence on who might be a supporter and who will oppose it.

> ➢ Shape the best strategy to grow from being just an idea to becoming a social technology that makes a difference.

> ➢ Define the first step and prepare contingency plans.

> ➢ Last but not least, design for the coherence of the result, once it's out there in the world.

Navigating may be done in a very short time, or stretched over a long period. It may overlap the reframing and/or the operationalizing phase, developing the necessary intelligence on-the-fly. Fit it to the situation. However, we find it is unwise to forget to spend time on it. Mostly there is no clear line between reframing and navigating except to say that the focus of the first is on creation and the focus of the second is on refining that creation before implementing too far on it.

This chapter is about the collective visioning and reflection we need to do in order to make wiser decisions as we operationalize the idea. We need to be clear together how we will navigate that option space and how others can follow our path. This chapter explores how relationships matter to this navigation and the scaling to come.

The idea might be huge, but we need to implement on it: together we create a project or organization given our emerging understanding of the reframe. To make it actionable, we look at different possible scenarios, prototyping it in our imagination, looking for potential pitfalls and noting upsides. As we navigate the options, we have found that the best social flows tend to arise from process hierarchies, which we explore later this chapter. We again look at how to nurture coherence during this phase because culture is the glue that holds us together as we begin to implement the idea. At the end, we provide a quick guide to use as you practice cultivating social flows in the navigating phase.

Why Relationships Matter

Fortunately, a mental space has no speed limit—unlike the physical world. Our thoughts can travel from one corner to another in the blink of an eye. We can explore any corner, scale any height using little energy. However, we do have other serious limitations: those set by our imagination, know-how, and experience. Our thoughts cannot travel beyond that, unless aided by others, or stimulated by other viewpoints, or unless we learn from someone else's experience.

Exploring a mental space is best done by a diverse network of people, willing to share their views and observations with each other. Connect the new frame with people, their ideas, and create relationships between them. Let them roam the valleys and heights of the new mental world, creating an ever more detailed map of options, paths, energy sources, and blocks. The more options the better: it will just make the navigation clearer and more complete. The desired side-effect is that more and more people carry the map in their mind, feel ownership of the new mental space, and contribute to the operationalization.

J

In late 2009, I had been noodling on the concept of 'thrivability'. I felt thrivability was a reframing of sustainability that actually could take us further, get us there faster, and open up new possibilities. I had been gathering pointers from a dozen friends, from just as many areas of interest that touched on thrivability. They advised me on how to move the concept (or meme) forward.

Two of them independently suggested to me that I gather short essays from a wide range of people into a little book on the topic. I had a small time window (90 days) before a good launch moment at SXSW Interactive, and few funds. First I asked a few people to pitch in some funds to cover my time commitment to producing it, which they generously did. Secondly, I started with page names for the book. I had been collaborating with a few people on a Thrivability game using a card deck that named some of the core components of thrivability. Many of those cards turned into titles for essays. I asked my ring of advisors to pick a word from the cards, and then write a <500-word essay.

The first essay to arrive was on <u>Efficiency</u>, written by <u>Jerry Michalski</u>. He pointed out that nature wasn't all that efficient and took strength from a certain amount of redundancy. Wait! That was not what I had been expecting at all! I was an efficiency freak! I had been proudly optimizing for efficiency since I was a small child. Yet, everything that Jerry was saying seemed right to me and right for thrivability. At that point, I knew the collective work was going to be much better than anything I could do alone. I was learning!

More essays came in. I posted to social media how excited and thankful I was. I would talk with a friend and wonder if they too could write something for the little "Thrivability Sketch." And they quickly did! Friends asked me if they could ask friends. I started with a ring of 12 and a vision for about 30. Two weeks before my deadline I looked up to discover that I was processing over 60 contributions. (What was that about efficiency? I think it met its nemesis, scope-creep, for that project! But I was flying high on my new, redundant, not-efficient wings.)

Some essays came about quickly and simply. I would reach out to someone whom I really admired and asked them to write about something they deeply knew and already talked frequently about. Many would ask what I wanted them to say about how their word related to thrivability. My reply was that "we are all making this up together so feel free to write about your own impression of the relationship." This gave people permission to fill the essay with their own ideas. And I expressed my gratitude: how much I appreciated their work on the topic. Before I knew it, their essay would be submitted.

Other times it would be less easy. Like when I would challenge someone to tackle an idea they were uncomfortable with, like "exclusion." A check-in with the author would find them struggling with the idea, turning it around and around to find an angle to approach writing. My work would be to bounce back alternative angles to keep them rolling. Once, our email exchange turned into the essay itself (Creativity by Joe Bill).

We pulled it off, together. Over 60 contributions of writing and art produced in less than 90 days, which launched at SXSW in 2010 with a participatory WDYDWYD (why do you do what you do) photography challenge. People still ask, "How did you do that so fast?" Looking back, it was one part building relationships beforehand, one part bringing out the best in people, and one part managing a production schedule.

The production piece relied on the use of a modified personal kanban to track everything visually in my workspace. A personal kanban has three columns: to do, doing, and done. I added columns for the phases of production: requested, received, edited, art, and signed contract. I worked 12+ hour days the whole time. However, it would not have been possible without the relationships with people (and theirs with their friends, in several cases). Relationships built over years that allowed me to surface and produce the wisdom in a booklet in short order. Let's also not forget the effort of each contributor over years of work and study to hone their ideas and concepts which can't even begin to be accounted for.

Together we put those connections and collective wisdom into one booklet that I hope everyone is proud of. It certainly put a stake in the ground for the field of thrivability. It is posted for free on slideshare.com and has been viewed over 30,000 times. It has led to invitations to places as far south as Melbourne, Australia, and as far north as Oslo, Norway. I feel everyone who contributed can confidently say they contributed to the field of thrivability, and many of them continue to use and champion the meme.

The _Thrivability Sketch_ shows that relationships matter. Not just between people, but also between ideas and information. Relationships define the system that arises out of the network: they make up the preferred paths for the flow of information, influence, memes, and transactions, and the flow of the feedback loops that reinforce or restrain the state.

Thrivability was a reframe, while the _Thrivability Sketch_ acted as a way of charting the possibilities: detailing, collectively, what to consider and parameters to work with in building a more thrivable world. The process of creating the sketch was in alignment with the design it generated, a collaboration of many different voices from across the world (5 continents) from different perspectives (scientists, investors, philanthropists, improv professionals, technologists, executives, tree climbers, academics, nonprofit leaders, and changemakers—among many others). There was economic, racial/ethnic, religious, age, and gender diversity. However, there was also a shared narrative about what thrivability aspires to be. While there is diversity in the final _Sketch_, there is also significant coherence.

Mutuality

Mutuality is a key issue in building and sustaining relationships, such as the ones that produced the _Sketch_. In this chapter we talk about connecting people to an idea for them to explore and to share information about it. The process has several explicit steps:

> ➤ Invite people to 'own' the option space so they can explore it and create within it—by modifying it, expanding it, building on it, qualifying it.

> ➤ Invite divergent conversations between them that allow for exploring unthought possibilities.

> ➤ Then turn the conversation toward convergence to weave back toward a shared narrative.

> ➤ Bring people back to a core, shared area to get resolution: the shared narrative, map, model, or framing of the topic.

The goal is to have people who are interested in the idea see and acknowledge their connection to others who share the idea. The resulting interaction creates an exchange:

> ➢ They mutually enrich their mind map of what is possible, of how to navigate the potential.

> ➢ They establish their dependencies, what their relationship should be when going further, and what their mutual benefit or motivation will be. They see where they might be able to contribute meaningfully.

In the end, they build a narrative which they mentally own together and the consequences of which they freely accept.

Freedom here means the opportunity to enter into (and leave) relationships voluntarily. We are dependent on others in highly specialized and wealthy societies, but are we free to choose and change our dependencies as we see fit? Can we choose relationships with people with whom we share a narrative? If we can both choose to stay or go, we call that a double opt-in relationship.

In the command-and-control mindset, the focus is on power over others, on reducing voluntary choices: how to force a certain desired result to become reality, how to force another party to comply with your narrative. The antagonist of this kind of power is defense: when command-and-control powers are competing, there is a need to defend interests, as there is a lot to lose. Action leads to reaction, the exercise of power leads to defense, both eat up energy in combating one another. The effect can be seen in meetings where people act as representatives of competing interests, assuming they are in a zero-sum game where one party's loss is the other party's gain.

The command-and-control mindset strives to reduce motives to a few rules or guidelines, aimed at controlling your output by pressing emotional buttons.

In any voluntary relationship, the focus is normally not on power-over ("I control your output") but on motivation ("your desire to contribute, share, and receive") and power-with. There is an implied context of mutual motivation as both parties want to see, understand, and accept the exchange in the two-sided relationship to make it work. Well-understood and accepted mutual motivation instigates the double-opt-in required to use our energy freely.

The most popular and simple (and abused) form of motivation is self-interest, as used in economic theory. "I benefit in tangible ways—either bodily, financial, or in some other objective way physically." Pay money, get results, or so it is said.

Another self-interest model that is routinely used is Maslow's hierarchy of needs. It has great traction but it does not hold up in practice. What often escapes attention is that Maslow could not prove in real-life experiments that his pyramid described how people actually behaved. Quite the opposite.

In considering mutual motivation it is wise to study other models and research that give a richer view of our humanity, such as:

➢ The data from the Maslow-inspired experiments (paid for by the US Army) led to the _Primary Social Motives_ (PSM) approach as researched by McClelland and others. PSM focuses on our basic internal needs. According to PSM the dominant motives are the need for Achievement, Affiliation, or Power. Most people have one or maybe two of these inner motives as dominant ones.

➢ Daniel Pink in _Drive: The Surprising Truth About What Motivates Us_, describes how multiple studies have shown that, in our working life, we are mainly motivated by Autonomy, Mastery, and Purpose; the ability to have choice in our actions, the ability to improve our own capabilities, and the need to find satisfaction in the why. The pre-condition is that we do not have to worry on a daily basis about financial survival and sustenance.

➢ Jonathan Haidt describes in his work _The Righteous Mind_ how we all have six moral senses. He compares these senses to tastebuds on the tongue that sense sweetness or acidity. The combination produces a specific taste that we may like or not like. And tastes differ. He argues that the same applies to these moral senses. A particular narrative or proposition may trigger multiple moral senses. The combination may feel "right" to you, or "repelling." Again, tastes differ between individuals.

The moral senses, as defined by Haidt, are:

➢ Care (prevent harm)

➢ Liberty (prevent oppression)

➢ Fairness (prevent cheating)

➢ Loyalty (prevent betrayal)

➢ Authority (prevent subversion)

➢ Sanctity (prevent degradation)

And last but not least, we are all experts on the fact that in everyday life powerful emotions like love, compassion, and a need for spiritual fulfillment shape our motivations.

Command-and-control gets things done, in some circumstances. But networks based on mutual motivation appear to be necessary for more mature and sophisticated levels of organizing society. Frederic Laloux asserts in his book _Reinventing Organizations_ that over time we humans have been able to grow from "wolfpacks" to self-steering groups and beyond, only because we have become more sophisticated in our understanding of the motivations that drive mutuality and cooperation. Education, research, accumulated experience, and wisdom slowly but steadily increase the number of people who surpass a certain level of understanding. It allows them to experiment with a more complex and subtle way of cooperating, leading to new types of organization that can accomplish new tasks and/or reach new heights. He distinguishes five levels:

> _Red_: tribal hierarchy dictatorships which divide labor and have commanding authority to navigate chaos. Gang-like.

> _Amber_: Formal hierarchy with stable, repeatable process. Military/government-like.

> _Orange_: Growth-oriented machine like organizations striving for innovation and operating on meritocracy. Corporation-like.

> _Green_: Shift from shareholder- to stakeholder-driven, focus on empowerment of members. Values-based organizations.

> _Teal_: Living, self-regulating organizations with evolutionary purpose. Likened to living organisms.

We found that being able to think in flows, to perceive the potential of mutual motivation in relationships is a prerequisite for building "Teal" type organizations.

The power of thinking in flows can be perceived when you start to explore the new reframe, when you need to build a map of the new world, to navigate through its wilderness.

Looking Ahead

Through our conversations we found that some mental prototyping of how things play out led to better outcomes later, as risks could be anticipated and worked with proactively rather than reactively. In the following pages we lay out several steps for creating conceptual prototypes. First use the list in the next section to get clear on what you need from the map. Second, build a tangible/visual arrangement of the concepts and hurdles. Third, play out some scenarios of what can happen. Fourth, look for phase changes and critical relationships in the way things might play out. Next look for how feedback can be used to help correct your course over time.

Mapping the New Territory Together

It is a great feeling when the consequences of a new idea—a reframe—dawn on you ("I get it!"). A block is removed, a wealth of fresh ideas becomes visible, hopes and dreams start to develop themselves. It is like setting foot in a new land. And, as with a new land, you would like to have a map of the territory before committing yourself to a path. Your resources are finite and it is better to have a course charted that you feel has the best chance of success.

Good maps and charts allow for good navigation: the development of a rich set of scenarios, strategies, and contingency plans to operationalize the dream in the next phase. In practice we see that the following list is what makes sense when moving into operationalizing an idea. So while technically this is the list for operationalizing, we have it here to clarify what the following pages and processes should lead to. In short, once you have the following, you probably have what you need to operationalize:

➢ The new reframing has been increased in strength by exploring it (as opposed to being weakened, with more doubts added)

- the risks feel assessed and addressed
- the first deliverable is fleshed out
- there are some contingency plans
- the resources to reach the first deliverable are within reach
- the navigational path seems clear
- there seems to be enough "defensive" capability available to engage the environment (depending on hostility of the environment), as in:
  o friends and followers, preferably in positions to make a difference

> o   answers to frequently asked questions and potential spreading of FUD (fear, uncertainty, and doubt)
>
> o   relevance of the new reframing to a broader group
>
> o   communication channels

So how do we get this list completed? To address the risks, lay out some contingency plans, and flesh out deliverables; it helps to prototype. We are not looking at all kinds of prototyping of ideas, we are specifically looking at those involved in social flows and the social technologies that enable them.

Make Your Maps Tangible Together

Good maps and charts allow for good navigation: the development of a rich set of scenarios, strategies, and contingency plans to operationalize the dream in the next phase.

The best methods for developing mental maps and mental navigation start with a collective process, with visual aids like moodboards, brown paper on the wall, big wooden chess pieces on the floor or a game played. The variety of tools is much bigger than these three, but they all have in common 1) physical representation and 2) collective interaction. There is something about looking at the same physical representation and making changes to it that provokes a fast creative interaction.

Moodboards: ask people to pin images to a board over the course of a week that they feel are associated with the common goal. No words or text, just images. After a week, group around the board and just ask people to place each image to either the "cool" side, or the "uncool" side, with a spoken explanation why they (dis-)like it. The reaction to each other's choices shows in 15 minutes where the consensus is, and where the dissent lies. The exercise preps everyone for an individual follow-up where they can verbalize their thoughts and issues, which would be much harder for them without the moodboard exercise. The exercise gives the subconscious mind room to express itself, and the conscious mind time to verbalize. Secondly, the collective process shows where there is consensus and where there are different opinions. The pitfall of this process is people who are consensus-seekers, who take an image and turn to the group and try to create consensus where to place it, cool or uncool ("Hey people, don't we all think that ...."). You need the unfiltered individual reaction.

Chess: in this exercise, sit in a circle and place big wooden chess pieces, sticks and blocks in the middle. The chess pieces represent, for instance, the goal ("the prize," the king), guardians and opponents. Sticks are boundaries: limits, hurdles, or assumptions. Blocks are resources. The prize is in the middle, surrounded by guardians and sticks. Opponents are in the field, as are resources. The first question is how people think the field is positioned, naming the items. The second is to verbalize what the "prize" is: a way to discover variations in what people expect as the reward, and if they are in conflict or not. In subsequent steps, discuss the sticks, name them, and decide if they are immovable or not. Decide what the opponents will try to do. All the while, rearrange the physical placement of items to represent the evolving mental map.

When technology is used to help people navigate complex arrangements, gamified versions help explore the map and the tech. The moodboard and chess pieces are simple enough to understand mentally, but complex arrangements require instant computations of interactions between multiple players. Our minds cannot handle that in real time, so tech has to come to the rescue. In Chapter 7 we explore this intricate issue of supporting tech in more detail.

Charting a Scenario in a Complex System

This work is not that of an artist creating a masterpiece of technical skill. Rather it is the art of making the connections, pathways, and options through immense complexity into something useful, so useful and easy to navigate that it fades from our attention, so we can focus on the work it enables.

The scenario part is not straightforward. Any complex system, like a group or society, can have many states and configurations. Some interventions lead to destructive self-reinforcing loops, some to thriving ecosystems, even within the same framework. The challenge is to aim for thrivability.

For instance, we are all familiar with the concept of the poverty trap: once you spend all your time just surviving from meal to meal it is almost impossible to pull yourself out of the hole. You miss one payment and have to pay interest and catch up, which you can't do without more income. Service fees and penalties accrue. You are stuck in a state which is destructive, yet getting out of it is nigh impossible. You need a new option or relationship to reverse that position. Even better than reversal is a societal design that prevents people from falling into the poverty trap in the first place.

So when reframing introduces new options and possibilities, you don't want them to turn into new destructive traps.

Conceptual Prototypes: Scenarios and Forecasts

We want to get a sense of how the reframe will take shape and interact with the world. Developing scenarios for how the reframe could play out might be a simple exercise or a lengthy one. No single way of developing scenarios is right for all cases. There are rigorous process methods like Scenario Planning, but common sense also goes a long way. Even having a process to use may include a ton of guesswork. It tends to be the fastest iteration that gets you somewhere rather than a lot of contemplating the initial idea. So it is okay to guess, but only if you follow that up by testing the guesswork: play out the guess in your head, test the scenario with others, and reiterate.

Paul Saffo offers *Six Rules for Effective Forecasting* to help reduce the errors many of us are prone to. Insightfully, he writes, "In forecasting, as in navigation, lots of interlocking weak information is vastly more trustworthy than a point or two of strong information." Saffo follows with, "The effective forecaster looks to history to find the rhymes, not the identical events."

There are many processes for imagining what can happen. Here are a few common approaches we see being used:

> ➢ The Delphi Method has been used for a half a century to gather expert opinions on possibilities in an iterative process to refine and converge on a forecast. Gather a group of experts on a diverse array of relevant topics and discuss what each may see and then develop some landmarks that seem probable in the timeframe being considered. This model is used by futurists like those at the Institute for the Future.

> ➢ Shell popularized Scenario Planning during the '70s as a result of the oil crisis. Scenario Planning generates several divergent scenarios, hoping to anticipate the cascade of impacts from a triggering event. The trick to doing useful scenarios, besides bringing together wildly different people, is coming up with an alternate world and seeing how things play out in that alternative. Scenario Planning is helpful when trying to imagine black swan event possibilities that would radically change the environment.

> ➤ Three Horizons invites us to notice how different people attend to, and are motivated by, short-, medium-, and long-term goals and vision. It is a more highly participatory visioning process that involves our stakeholders and moves us to relevant action together. Neither Delphi nor Scenario Planning tend to engage the various stakeholders in their process, where Three Horizons does.

Nassim Nicholas Taleb explains how traders look at scenarios: risks and opportunities are often not nicely and evenly distributed in the bell-curves that we are shown in Statistics 101. Rather we find that they are highly asymmetric. Traders will avoid options that have a high probability of a small positive outcome and a low probability of a very negative outcome, unless they can insure against the negative. Instead, they look for scenarios that have a low probability of a very positive outcome and a high probability of a small negative outcome. They prepare to absorb or compensate the negative outcome, and then they try many times until they eventually hit the jackpot. Venture capitalists do the same thing. In R&D you try quickly as many approaches as you can afford in order to find the right one.

You may want to create scenarios connected with worst possible outcomes or best possible outcomes. Or you might be more concerned with what outcomes have a high probability. What you want from the scenario will shape which method you use and where you take it. What is critical is getting clarity about what is motivating your choice of which scenarios to develop. One key we learned through practice and conversations with practitioners is that the method you use needs to fit the scope of the intended impact. In resource terms, apply 10-15% of the time or money available to this part of the process. Consider it an investment in saving resources later. We also prefer engaging stakeholders since they often have surprising and highly relevant wisdom.

To set up possible scenarios or forecasts we have to ask ourselves several questions:

> ➤ What is the timeframe we are considering?

> ➤ Who are the stakeholders and what are their motivations/drivers?

> ➤ What is the current flow trending toward?

> ➤ What might be critical uncertainties?

The common sense approach relies on searching for the "unthinkable," for the basic assumptions you or others take for granted, for sacred cows that are untouchable. The most interesting scenarios are the ones where a basic assumption is overthrown, or a sacred cow is slaughtered. Suddenly the impossible may become possible.

The assumption or sacred cow can be your own or it can be something which limits your own view of options you have. Or it can be a weak point in the frame you want to replace: an assumption that is the foundation of a way of organizing our society.

Exploring these cornerstones is fun when you are in a safe environment, in a group that enjoys pushing the envelope, allows for seemingly outrageous ideas, and is willing to go along for the sake of it, just to see where that crazy idea will lead us. Invite some intelligent "crackpots," outliers, fringe inhabitants: you may be surprised by what they trigger.

Both Delphi and Scenario Planning rely on the quality and variation of the people brought together. If you are working on significant financial opportunities, these are good methods for considering what might impact your business. If you want to think through the phasing of flows over time or deeply engage stakeholders, then Three Horizons may be most useful. If you are working in a community or in a group where financial flows are less involved, then a more casual ideating session may be sufficient. If you are working in multi-sector collaboration, you may want to employ several forecasting and scenario planning processes as both a conceptual prototyping exercise and an onboarding to the reframe process.

Design Choices

Phase Change and Critical Relationships

We do not set out here to make you instant futurists. We do want to provide just enough to get you started imagining different paths ahead in the idea space and point out crucial pieces to consider before you do some conceptual prototyping. To explore these ideas further, look to CultivatingFlows.com to dig deeper or contribute your wisdom.

As we build out possibilities, the question arises, what to look for? As we studied practitioners who are having a transformational effect in selecting scenarios, we discovered that they focused on the critical relationships that keep a system either locked in a certain state, or cause sudden transitions when crossing a threshold: in other words, phase change.

To help ground this abstract process, let's look at a dynamic in nature that can be used as a conceptual guide, in a biomimicry sense. <u>Prof. Marten Scheffer</u> of Wageningen University in the Netherlands studies complex systems in biology and society. One of his famous experiments is about lakes. He observed that lakes could turn from being clear to being green with algae in a very short time, without much warning. The challenge was to find the critical relationship in the ecosystem that caused the sudden transition and try to reverse it. He succeeded by removing all the fish from a lake that had turned green from algae. It broke a core feedback loop in the ecosystem which allowed the lake to restore itself and become clear again. Putting even more fish back in the lake after the transition did not break the stability of the ecosystem: the lake stayed clear.

Once we have a sense of how the space might play out, then we can begin to make a conceptual prototype for it. When working on a conceptual prototype, look for those critical relationships that have important positive feedback loops, like the lake does. By positive here, we mean that more of something triggers even more of it. These are usually balanced with other feedback loops[2] that work in the opposite direction as well, or you end up with too much—algae, in the case of the lake.

Navigating, then, is the conscious effort to enhance the desired outcome and reduce the chance of unwanted outcomes by introducing social technology. Finding the critical relationships in a system helps: it helps to discover how to disrupt them as Marten Scheffer did, or to design a new one that changes the behavior of the system.

All social technology development (for social flow) works within complex adaptive systems because it involves humans, who learn and change over time. Human networks are complex—in that we have a dynamic network of interactions—and adaptive in that we learn and change all the time. Because of the complexity and change involved, there are no simple best practices that work every time. No fallback, default paths to success with social technology and flows. Charting the path to the preferred options is much more an art than a science: hard to predict its outcome, in practice, but very much worth the effort to try, learn, and adapt.

And tools that help you to navigate through this wilderness help a lot.

---

[2] In the lake example, the positive feedback loop to keep a lake clear is as follows: a clear lake allows plants to grow, plants that give hiding places to small creatures from the fish that feed on them; these small creatures eat the algae to keep the lake clear. A green lake prevents sunlight reaching plants, so there is no hiding place and the creatures get eaten by fish, so the algae can flourish.

Feedback: Catering for Human Intuition

The challenge to parties exploring what is possible, is to see and understand the mutuality. It is easy to show mathematically that the richness of possibilities explodes as more relationships are made possible, as more people become related. The drawback is clear: the hard part for each actor is to assess the potential of all the direct and indirect interactions he or she is part of. While we will go into feedback in depth in Part 4, a quick exploration is worthwhile here.

The new idea or reframe creates a new space, and navigating is about finding our path through that new space together. As practitioners, we want to be aware of concerns that come up. Where is the resistance? What is the tension to notice and surf? The drawback of adding options and new relationships is that choice anxiety may result: so many options, so many scenarios to explore. Simplification by excellent navigation is a powerful tool to overcome the fear of overwhelming choice and the resulting organizational paralysis too. The power of IT systems can be harnessed to make navigating a complex option space easy in practice. For example, we can use software to present only two or three options at a time in a series of questions, refining the choice set. Even a restaurant menu uses graphic design to help us manage the overwhelm of choice by segmenting meal courses or main ingredients.

We humans can deal very well with fast feedback loops that predict what the effects of a choice will be, where we can play with the parameters, play with preferences, and test some outliers. We don't need to see the choices as much as we need to see the consequences of those choices. "Should I turn left or right?" is a less good question than telling my mapping software where I want to end up and how I want the route to be optimized—and asking it how to get there.

The social designs we create need to provide simple feedback for participants to ride or surf rather than all the data and complicated manuals that go into computing the tensions they are navigating. We don't learn physics in order to ride a bicycle. We learn what balance feels like and how fast we have to go to keep upright. Whenever possible, keep choice options available at the balance level that people can see or feel and not at the level of physics or the technical manual. Thus participants in the flow can best modulate their own behavior (and the behavior of others) to help keep the whole system working.

Feedback is Navigation

Good navigation of the new reframe wraps up the complexity in simple feedback loops where you can learn to "ride" the space. You just have to know what "balance" looks like. For thrivability, the simple question: "does this generate more value than it consumes?" enables decent course correction. For wirearchy, the signal might be about whether it involves power-over or power-with. In the roundabout, it is the simple principle of ceding to oncoming flow and looking other drivers in the eye. No one has to calculate, consciously, the speed of the vehicles or the risks of collision. Navigation is about goal-seeking, using trial and—reading from the feedback indicator—error to find the balance of flow, rather than taking over steering through control.

J *Recently, I attended a workshop on walkable cities. The walkable city is a reframe on the prior model, which in hindsight we could call the "drivable city." Having the new reframe then, we have to drill down into specifics. What does a walkable city mean? How would you know one if you saw it? We toured a neighborhood and asked:*

➢ *Who has this been designed for?*

➢ *Who was not included in the considerations?*

➢ *What activities were being encouraged and which were being discouraged?*

➢ *Who would feel like they belonged here?*

➢ *What would make it more useful and enjoyable for pedestrians, cyclists, and the handicapped?*

We looked at how the roads intersected with sidewalks. We considered how one intersection forced pedestrians to walk across five lanes of moving cars to get to the other side and another intersection where there were buffers for pedestrians to pause safely. We looked at signage. And we looked for elements that give a sense of aliveness and welcoming—planters, artwork, sitting areas.

A walkable city provides clues and feedback that we humans can grasp intuitively. We want to use visual cues rather than explicit directions. Red, orange, or yellow lights and paint indicate caution. In their book *Nudge*, Cass R. Sunstein and Richard H. Thaler explain how, on the curve of Lake Shore Drive in Chicago, the road is painted with white lines that trick drivers into feeling they are going faster than they really are. This nudges people into driving more slowly. It works better than the suggested speed sign.

Intuition:	understanding without needing a rational explanation

Human intuition is enormously powerful. We do well with things we can't rationally understand. We humans have some incredible capabilities, almost from the moment we are born. Like a sense for music and rhythm. In his TEDx talk in Amsterdam, researcher Henk Jan Honigh asked us to sing collectively a line from a 1980s' pop song, without any reference or clue. He played the original afterwards, and the key and the rhythm were very close to our singing. Apparently, it is an anomaly if someone can't do that. We didn't all have to learn it formally. He even showed that we could guess more or less the language of the mother from the sounds her baby makes, if we are familiar with that language.

Young children quickly learn to ride a bicycle. We can run and catch a flying baseball. Walking through a crowded city without bumping into others? No problem. Driving cars on highways, at speeds over 60 mph with less than a second distance? Common skill. Seeing even tiny deviations in a straight black line: anybody can do that. Yet memorizing a string of 10 digits is a task most people fail at, and computers find easy. The trick is to design for these human capacities and intuitions.

Designing tools for navigating the option space requires a conscious effort to cater for our innate strengths while compensating for our weaknesses. Create feedback loops in navigation that enable course-correcting by participants in the flow. When you clarify what that feedback loop is, everything seems suddenly clear. Figuring out that loop can be complicated. Here are some tips we learned in practice:

➢ What is the core value that drives the idea and how can you recognize it in action (e.g. thrivability, wirearchy)?

➢ What might some hear, smell, touch, or taste that lets them know they are on track (e.g. walkability)?

➢ What might behavioral economics say about how people really work in relation to this idea, as it is practiced (e.g. the lines on Lake Shore Drive)?

Navigation Quality is Driving the Trade-off Between Richness and Ease of Use

The new reframe might create new options, which is great, but the drawback is that people may get choice anxiety. They may feel overwhelmed by too many options, so much to decide. They may feel uncertain about the outcome and be afraid of missing a better option.

This is fundamental. The richer the option space, the more local "valleys and hills" there are in the option space. This variety may obscure better solutions further away. The work of <u>Stuart Kauffman</u> and others shows that there is a tough trade-off between richness and complexity. You need to limit the richness to get a finite solution space. The limit is ripe when you still have a space which is understandable and navigable for humans. The converse is also true: the better the navigation, the richer the option space complexity can be.

A combination of clever design and strong IT systems will do the trick for navigation systems. If you choose primary drivers that people can recognize as their own, and let IT calculate the resulting indicators of the effects of these choices, people will start to play around and navigate to the choice of their liking. The combination gives incredible customization, empowered and driven by participants and customers.

Take for instance financial planning. It's hard to understand, as so many factors come into play. In many European countries you can expect a state-supplied minimum pension, and income from collective pension funds and insurance funds. You may have your own capital, possibly tied up in a house. Inheritances may come into play, you may want to help your children when they start to work, you may want to retire a little bit earlier. All within complex tax rules. Instead of relying on (expensive) advisors to guide people to a choice, experiments have been done in the Netherlands with a navigation tool. The tool takes the basic financial input parameters of a family, and allows that family to play around with the most important life choices they have, and the most important external parameters like inflation and interest rates. The tools calculate the effect on net income over the years to come, and the effect on the family's capital position over time. Finally, it presents the information in an easy-to-read graph.

The researchers found that most people could zoom in easily on what they thought was their best option, just by trial and error and seeing the effects on the results. At the layer of individuals, people can adjust to fit their goals using feedback they can understand. At the collective level, more people can be flowing into a future they want, putting less pressure on government resources as a result of poor forecasting by individuals.

Process Hierarchy as a Powerful Design Principle

When navigation has shown potential paths forward, a rough design sketch will be drawn and explored. How to implement the idea, how to bring the narrative to operational impact?

The pitfall of this phase is that we are so trained in our education to think in functional hierarchies (machine-like), that we can only begin to consider this kind of design. We found that there is more, and excitingly more.

Functional hierarchy is how we design machines; process hierarchy is how life is organized. The use of biomimicry in social technology is to apply the ideas of process hierarchy to social flows.

The difference between a process hierarchy and a functional hierarchy can be demonstrated by a simple example. Someone is entrusted with the security of the building and has the authority to make decisions about who to allow in, based on rules. In a functional/power hierarchy the boss/CEO can step in and overrule on the spot ("this is an exception"). In a process hierarchy he cannot break the process. He can change the rules of the process for everyone, but not overrule the instance through positional power.

Jean is working with a client who wants to expand operations. The client does not want to create more bureaucracy nor managers as they scale, which they perceive as bottlenecks to workflow. They are looking at how to develop process hierarchies along with guiding principles so that any participant in their network will act in ways that are acceptable to the organization as long as they follow the principles and respect the processes. There is something soothing in working in a process hierarchy, as you can anticipate what the expectations are. In a hierarchy like those found in traditional industrial organizations, we are at the mercy of those in positional power who may or more likely may not convey guiding principles and clear expectations.

We spoke at length with **Ton van Asseldonk**, a passionate practitioner of putting process hierarchy in place to unlock new social technology. His motto is to give us back the agency and choice that was taken from us by industrialization. He argues that event-driven systems are enabled by process hierarchy to give us the heterogeneity we need. This is something industrial-designed organizations simply can't do. The following paragraphs are highly indebted to his work and conversations with him, which he gracefully allowed us to use. While his work is primarily in the for-profit sector, we believe his insights and strategies can be applied more broadly.

We need energy, goods, and services to lead our lives as we desire. Each of us strives to improve our own life, and the lives of our loved ones and family. We are the economy, as we create demand by living our lives.

Throughout history you see a lot of experimentation with how to meet these needs and cater for improvement. Specialization helped a lot to increase productivity, which reduced the cost of existing goods, which in return made room for us to get more/better/different products/services. Trade and money and markets increased the accessible trading space for specialists and allowed the concentration of capital. Collectives such as a corporation or an institution or nation created the size and scale to make deep and risky investments with huge potential payoffs. The freedom to start offering new products and services accelerated the development, giving us the breadth and wealth of what can be offered to us.

As usual, each improvement and step forward creates its own drawback. The step to industrialize manufacturing created a massive reduction in costs, sure. But it came at the expense of individual choice. "Any color as long as it is black." Jump forward a century and you can observe that the industrial model has been applied to services as well, even where it does not bring as much benefit as with products.

At the same time, we (the economy) want to go beyond "cheap but standard, as designed by someone else." The better life now seems to be found by moving in the direction of much more individualization for the same price: individualization of products, of energy, of services, by going beyond the industrial model.

In discussions on quality we are accustomed to believing that the only option we have is a tradeoff: higher quality means higher costs of services and/or products. But quality should be read as "meeting our individual needs and desires," or "fit for purpose" much more than "well built."

The source of this belief is our experience with industrial organizations which are designed to deliver a large amount of the same semi-standard services or products for low costs. A pre-designed product or service (for instance a medical "protocol" for treatment of a specific ailment) is a Procrustean bed: either it is minimal and leads to low costs but under-delivers for many, or it is richly defined with higher costs and is over delivering for many. Support for heterogeneity of what is delivered is needed to get out of this trap.

But productivity collapses in industrial organizations when heterogeneity increases (for instance, in care or in education). This is because an industrialized organization is designed to combine:

1. A limited number of solutions.

2. An easy to navigate solution space (time/costs to search and find good/best solution) because of the limited number of solutions.

3. High volume to make the high costs and time delays of top-down designing and setting up the solutions affordable, because these costs are amortized over the volume.

Heterogeneity in industrial organizations runs into a brick wall:

1. Heterogeneity requires a rich solution space with many solutions.

2. The rich solution space is more costly to navigate (time/money to search and find good/best solution).

3. The number of units per solution decreases, so the high costs and time delays of top-down design and setting up solutions must be borne by a limited number of customers, increasing the price.

The way to support heterogeneity is to step away from the top-down industrial setup and create ENE processes in a process hierarchy.

Emergent means that the (heterogeneous, diverse) solutions emerge from the ad-hoc combination of individual steps and building blocks (processes). Instead of predefined solutions, only the boundaries and rules are designed: anything that abides by the boundaries and rules is an acceptable solution, the choice of how to combine them lies with the customer, user, or participant.

The building blocks are combined in networked processes. A network is not a linear or hierarchical structure; a network allows for multiple pathways, redundancy in routes, turning back to previous points, feedback loops and so on. The increased connectivity hugely increases the available range of what is possible.

Event-driven processes, by definition, are about reacting to events, like choices by the customer/user or other triggers (like elevated blood sugar levels or elapsed time).

The process hierarchy then describes how building blocks are designed, maintained, and innovated for.

Use Case: ENE in Care Brabant

The industrialization of healthcare is exemplified by standardized protocols for each ailment, with corresponding financial compensations paid out by insurance companies. Each protocol is designed with a trade-off, usually on the safe side. This means that in around 75% of the cases there is some degree of overtreatment and wasted costs as a result; in the remaining 25% of cases, underperformance in what is delivered.

Its gets worse when people have multiple ailments. Unfortunately, in reality, diabetes (for instance) correlates with obesity, cardiac problems, and problems with joints and muscles. Older people tend to have a complex list of problems. Inside a hospital there is some flexibility to adapt to the individual's needs; but it gets problematic when people are living at home and receive some care at home, and then have to go to their doctor at the hospital for check-ups and tests.

The combination of multiple standardized protocols can become both very expensive and very uncomfortable for the patient.

An event-driven process has been designed and implemented to overcome this stalemate. A group of over 300,000 patients in the south of the Netherlands gets fully individualized treatment processes which are custom-made from predefined atomic processes, selected by the patient and the professional caring for them. So, if someone is living in the countryside and has problems with traveling, a choice can be made to make most visits at their home. And if a check-up has to be done in the hospital, all checks for all ailments are combined in the same trip. Routine checks, for instance of blood sugar levels, blood pressure, etc. can trigger a more thorough check. The exact moment and best timing of the combined tests is left to the patient and the professional.

Designing systems as process hierarchies rather than as functional hierarchies (who has positional power?) allows us to design and maintain complex systems with rich behavior, without succumbing to the overwhelming task of trying to lock down, command-and-control everything in detail.

Coherence for Navigating

Metaphorically, reframing can be seen like discovering and exploring a new territory for the first time. Scouts and expeditions venture into uncharted areas, unfazed by the uncertainty of opportunity or risk. They bring back knowledge of rich and fertile land, and of treacherous swamps and unscalable heights.

The act of sharing the discovery builds the shared story of how to travel to the first homestead.

Navigating is the next step: you build a map together like cartographers do; it points out good trails and shows where signposts and other markers can be found. Your map might come from a group exercise with post-its or blocks or from discussing the boundaries and qualities of the space. The map and navigation tools help people who are interested in the new territory to get up to speed quickly, to contribute faster, to be able to scale out the process of discovery.

You play around with possible infrastructure designs, placing future cities in the map and deducing from that where roads and bridges are needed.

This is a nice metaphor, but it fails in demonstrating the major difference between the discovery of a territory and the discovery of a new mental space created by a reframe.

Like we said before, a mental space has no speed limit, unlike the physical world. Our thoughts can travel from one corner of the mental space to another in the blink of an eye. However, unlike the physical world, we cannot think about what we cannot imagine. Enlarging our personal mental space can only be done by others who share their mental space, when we are stimulated by other viewpoints, when we learn from someone else's experience. And the other way around. Use tangible objects to help share mental space and prototype together.

The pitfall of navigating is that the early discoverers fall into the role of leaders who know the territory, who have already created a design, know the intended outcome and are guiding others to join the big plan. It limits the development of the shared mental space, it forgets the lesson that a lot of motivated people who search in a distributed but cooperative way for solutions are consistently quicker and more creative than a small number "at the top" can be. The whole idea of "Teal" organizations is to allow shared power to come into full bloom.

Coherence in this phase is about finding a balance between embracing diversity and allowing the conditions for this powerful distributed search to exist on one hand, and keeping focus on progress and getting things done on the other hand.

In the example of "Lean and Green" in Chapter 1, the support organization of the community is consciously and deliberately positioning itself as a servant to the process, while formally it owns the brand and the copyright, sets the standards, initiates communication and meetings, and acts as a spokesperson for the community. It could easily morph into "The Management" of the program, but that is a trap, a dead-end street.

Thought leaders and senior members are asked to become ambassadors for the program, and collectively invited to act as a steering group that gives strategic direction. Frontrunners in the community are invited collectively to comment on the proposed development of the standards and guidelines, to give guidance on priorities, to agree upon what should be changed and added. This is in the form of meetings with 15-20 people who actively voice their thoughts, ideas, and concerns. The unwritten rules are that proposals by non-members (including the support organization) must be supported by the ambassadors and the leading members before they become accepted. And that proposals and criticisms by members are taken very seriously. This has led, over the years, to a vibrant community and continuous development of the program, quite often triggered by the members themselves with creative ideas. In contrast, competing initiatives that were designed with a command-and-control mindset have not succeeded.

As more people are attracted, we also need to be mindful of what the protocols for interacting are. We are not as rational as we would like to believe ourselves to be. We don't obviously find the best solution and then implement it. We have egos, blind spots, cultural differences, beliefs, and personalities that influence the choices we make. Some people feel a need to be in a position to tell others what to do. Some may have a hidden agenda, wanting to exploit the value generated. We need processes for exploring and sharing to be effective. Freedom to enter into mutual relationships requires assistance and protection. The value of good process in this phase is in providing the safety, security, and caring required.

Motives

Let's consider more deeply how motives play a role in coherence. Motivation is the mental energy source for people to make the effort, join the flow to develop the reframe and navigation, and take the next steps: the energy source needed to tackle problems, accept challenges, and face adversity.

In our research we were struck by how vast the variety of motives is that people can have, in various combinations, and changing in importance over time. At the same time people find it hard to accept and understand other motivations than their own, tend to think theirs is the right one, and unconsciously move towards more homogenous subgroups. The pitfall is to move to a monoculture that becomes vulnerable to groupthink.

H *Earlier in my career I joined a company that had previously prided itself on its sophisticated recruitment process for new staff. Psychological profiles were established and used for selection purposes.*

It seemed great, until management realized that they had painted themselves into a corner by focusing on one particular profile. They lacked the outliers and creative people who could deal with a new and unexpected change in the market. Company staff were similar in profile and motivation, with the same competences and shortcomings. Their deficiencies had even been reframed as a positive trait, based on the success of the company: "this is how we are." Outliers who were hired became isolated and were not promoted (organizational immune system), because their peers mainly identified that they were not as good at the competences they themselves excelled in. It took a lot of time and consistent management attention to introduce diversity that would stick.

When we discuss coherence in each chapter it is about how to foster diversity, how to cater for various kinds of motivation while sharing a common goal. You can only travel mentally to places you can imagine: diversity increases the number and variety of such places that you can imagine together.

When we discuss mutuality as a binding force it is also about the motivation to share and cooperate.

The biggest pitfall in thinking about motives is to simplify our rich and complex human existence down into a few rules or guidelines, or into just one of the theoretical and empirical models for motivations that are available. There are many, each of which captures a different part of that richness.

The narrative of the reframe can't be all things to all people. As we said in "Narrative," it describes or implies roles. These roles fit with the internal narratives people have about themselves. Some people will be more attracted than others to the narrative and the roles in the narrative; some might even be repelled. Someone who craves power and is in a position of power will not like a narrative that results in less power and status for themselves.

Whatever motivates people about a new reframe, from the (negative) frustration of what has not been working to the (positive) power and visibility of being an early participant in the new, it may not maintain their motivation through the lifespan of the endeavor. We noticed that it is important to allow for the handover of (implicit) leadership and participation, to invite those who are motivated by a particular phase of development or by the specific change that is envisaged—rather than nurture people whose motivation is simply tied to "doing something new." Thinking of phases of development, it is clear that some of us love the high-risk adventure of new ideas while others thrive in the steady growth of a well-tested and proven idea.

Sometimes the motivation comes before the new reframe (as is often the case if a team forms to create a reframe). Sometimes the reframe comes and then the team emerges around it. In either case, notice what is motivating participation and honor that. We found working against motivations to be useless. Work with people's motivation to find and build the enthusiasm for moving forward. As in the story of Lean and Green, leave the curmudgeons out of it. Find where the energy is and build on it.

Navigating: Conclusion

Navigating consists of exploring the new space and developing the best approach for how to achieve the dream. In the navigation phase, we expand the community participating in the evolution of the idea, gathering intelligence on who supports it, who resists it, and why. This involves creating mutuality where there is a sense of shared ownership of the idea and we understand the motives driving everyone. It helps to do some forecasting, using Delphi, Scenario Planning, Three Horizons or another futurist process to play out the idea over time. This enables us to create conceptual prototypes. When working on a conceptual prototype, look for those critical relationships that have important positive feedback loops, like the lake does. By positive here, we mean that more of something triggers even more of it. These are usually balanced with other positive feedback loops that work in the opposite direction as well, or you end up with too much—algae, in the case of the lake. We test these prototypes asking questions like: what is the current trend and what are critical uncertainties we face as risks? For social flows, we also look for phase changes and critical relationships in our scenarios. Then we design for people as humans, leveraging human intuition to make navigation by the next layer of participants easier. We shape the idea based on the map we create of the options and how it influences the ecosystem. Designing for both richness of the space and ease of use, we need to choose our errors. Finally, we formulate contingency plans to make the idea more secure.

As throughout the book, be sure to check the website to dive deeper into practitioner stories and interviews. And come back often as we continue to expand. Contribute your own! We invite you to share what you have learned in practicing this phase by joining us on CultivatingFlows.com.

Quick Guide to Navigating

What we learned from our conversations with practitioners and from our own practice are a few key steps in Navigating:

Play out the idea in your head and with others. Really testing it will save time and energy later on.

Expand community, gather intelligence on advocates and resistors, shape the strategy and develop contingency plans.

Cultivate relationships and design for mutuality.

Use divergent conversation to explore the possibilities and convergent conversation to refine and come to a resolution.

Charting Scenarios:

> Scenario Planning, Delphi, Three Horizons, casual methods can be used.

> Depth of process should reflect investment and scope of stakeholders.

> Consider what the process should help you understand before choosing which process to use. Risk? Black swans? Resistance? Unintended consequences? Hurdles? Needs? Critical uncertainties?

> What are critical relationships (ones that can trigger phase changes)?

> Really notice relationships—between people, ideas, actions, and behaviors.

Mapping the Territory Together:

> Create small next steps that make it more real and tangible, building many successes leading toward a larger goal.

> The key to self-navigation is to have a tool that gives feedback quickly. Set the right pace for adjustments. Humans are extremely proficient in fast, iterative goal-seeking.

> Set limitations right. When we redesign the option space, it can appear complicated to everyone; so creating navigable paths, preferences, and default values (or limits) to choices makes the work more approachable.

Process Hierarchy wins over Functional Hierarchy:

> An Emergent, Networked, Event-driven (ENE) process is, for example, a process hierarchy.

> Authority is placed in the process not in a person who wields positional power.

> Industrial processes do not produce "customization" or manage heterogeneity well. By atomizing production and creating navigation pathways and process hierarchies, ENEs win.

> Navigation quality is the key to ENE success.

Coherence

> Coherence in this phase is about the balance between embracing diversity and allowing the conditions for the powerful distributed search to exist on one hand, and keeping focus on progress and getting things done on the other hand. Don't become a manager.

> Let people self-select those who have a shared narrative. There is a danger of exhaustion and stagnation in trying to reach full consensus, so don't waste energy on pulling in the stragglers.

> Stimulate co-ownership while keeping the ship together.

> Because power dynamics can derail these projects, it is important to find neutral territory for different interests to convene. Nurture a sense of safety, security, and caring.

> Be mindful of the motives of people engaging in order to encourage diversity of motivation thus increasing the resilience of the idea over its lifespan.

PART THREE:
OPERATIONALIZE

Introduction to Part Three

Operationalizing the reframe has many parts. Before we dive into Part Three, we want to clarify how operationalizing a social flow or using a social technology requires a different mindset than working with physical technology. From there, we go into the triggers that tell us we are ready to implement on the reframe or idea. We again clarify some ways that social flows differ from traditional approaches, including the engagement of stakeholders in the process of creation and how new social flows might differ from what Henry Mintzberg defined in 1979. We then explore organizational hybrids, some useful distinctions on scaling, and touch on decentralized organizations as innovative models of cooperative productivity. Finally, we clarify the facets of operationalizing we will explore in the following chapters. While this is only the introduction to Part Three, this clarification on operationalizing seemed dense enough to provide a quick guide, at the end, as well.

Form and Flow Drive Operationalization

We introduced the idea of social technology in Chapter 1 as tools to enable us to implement ideas about how to cooperate as humans. Cooperation is needed to get something done beyond what an individual can achieve alone. Social technology contrasts with physical technology, which is the implementation of ideas about how to co-opt (or cooperate with) matter in order to perform a function.

Social technology is entirely different from physical technology, especially when it comes to operationalizing.

In physical technology you take the laws of physics to model how the cooperation of physical items and energy will work. You design a structure with parts, define the relationships between the parts (functional hierarchy), and describe the process that is triggered by inputs. Build and test, refine, and maintain. Complicated, but for the most part reproducible.

In social technology you start with humans and their motivation, and how that influences cooperation or conflict. You look at human strengths (like assessment of trust) and weaknesses (like memorizing dull rows of data). You take into account that people learn, grow, and change through experience and age. You use previous experiences with forms of cooperation to build new ones. Physical technology plays a role in augmenting our strengths and compensating for our weaknesses. In social technology, we are part of what we cultivate, starting with planting a seed, cultivating its growth, and its mutation throughout generations. This is a complex, adaptive process—not all that easy to predict or replicate.

It is very tempting to take what we comfortably know, re-apply the language of physical technology, re-use its proven methods of solving design problems, and manage the operationalization phase accordingly. Yet that is a trap, a big trap, one we have struggled with time and again ourselves. We had to invent our own vocabulary to get out of the struggle.

The physical technology words "structure" and "protocols" are widely used in association with organizations. We have found they draw us back into the mechanical metaphor. For social flows, our mental image is more like life: you can identify an entity like a living cell by its boundaries, but that is an incomplete view. Without observation of the flow of matter and information and energy through the boundary and inside the cell you miss the essence. The smallest building block in social flows is an individual being instead of a cell, but the idea is the same. Individual living cells cooperate as well, which lets organs emerge. The boundary of an organ is visible but again the picture becomes more complete once the flow inside the organ and through the boundary is taken into account. And so on, viewing more complex emerging entities as we take bigger ensembles into account. Life works with emergent process hierarchies like this.

Our language lacks good words that describe what is important in this metaphor. We have chosen "Form" to describe the shape of the entity and the behavior of entities at its boundary, and "Flow" to describe the movement through the boundary between entities and within entities.

Form is about the boundary. Entities have boundaries that can be identified, that define outside and inside. Entities have a shape often based on the internal parts and their relationships, and on the interactions with equivalent forms. Entities can cooperate to let a new entity emerge, again with a boundary, a recursive view. Entities have intent. The entity takes a form that shapes its possibilities and opportunities.

Flow is the word for describing how information (including emotions and, sometimes, energy and matter) is flowing through boundaries and is flowing inside entities, and how that influences what comes next, triggers reactions, and gives direction to growth and learning.

Form and flow may be confused at first sight with an organizational structure: the main difference is that the observed patterns are an emergent result, not a top-down design.

We also use "governance" rather than "management" because more optimal social flows and forms tend to be self-regulating rather than hierarchically managed and controlled. Governance is how emergent entities grow and change, how they adapt to new intent or to changing conditions.

Governance is a lot about handling conflicts and dilemmas. We see conflicts and dilemmas as drivers of growth, in an anti-fragile[3] manner. They indicate tensions that arise from deeper causes, worthy of investigating and solving.

An attack is a different thing; it is not a conflict in this sense. You need defense against attacks intended to destroy the integrity of the entity, to take its freedom for intent away. You need resources and an immune[4] system to survive the attacks.

The next three chapters are about operationalizing flows, using this vocabulary. Operationalizing is such a rich and rewarding subject that we can only scratch the surface. We have left out a lot of details and explorations and created our website to continue adding to the body of knowledge. Here we have tried to capture in broad strokes how social flow entities differ from more traditional organizations.

It is time to start thinking about form, flow, and governance along with the tools to support them.

The Triggers to Operationalize

In theory, the three steps that we have so far identified in cultivating social flows (Reframing, Navigating, Operationalizing) are cleanly sequential. In practice, it is more like everything else in life: anything but linear and well-defined. The blurry boundary between Navigating and Operationalizing is a good example.

---

3 Nassim Taleb defines anti-fragility as the opposite of fragile: getting stronger by being hurt. Like muscles that get miniscule tears through exercise and react by growing more muscle, or getting an inoculation with a weak variant of a deadly virus, which teaches your immune system to defend itself against the real deal.

4 Taking the metaphor further, you can observe autoimmune diseases in entities. Immature democracies can suffer from confusing conflict with an attack. The result is that the winning 52% starts to suppress the losing 48%.

In most communities, there are some people who cannot wait to rush into action: "Just start, and we will make up things as we go!" Opposed to them are people who want to study and prepare more, and more, and more, before putting a toe in the water. The first group risks going straight into a dead-end, triggering aggressive pushback before they are ready, or finding that they lack a contingency plan. The second group may lose momentum and energy by delaying too long the decision to get started.

What we found in practice is that it's actually the group between them that usually tips the balance: as more people begin to get impatient and the group that wants to get into action increases, any event can trigger the avalanche: the ones that want action will pull the hesitating group along. So how do we know when to stop preparing and start converging?

Some people have an explicit checklist, others rely on experience or just gut-feeling. We said in Navigating that you want to aim to have this list completed in order to start operationalizing. We provide it again, here, as a reminder that in our research we have found it important to have the following in place before operationalizing:

➤ The new reframing has been strengthened by exploring it (as opposed to being weakened, with more doubts added):

- the risks feel assessed and addressed

- the first deliverable is fleshed out

- there are some contingency plans

- the resources to reach the first deliverable are within reach

- there seems to be enough "defensive" capability to engage the environment (depending on hostility of the environment), as in:

  o friends and followers, preferably in positions to make a difference

  o answers to frequently asked questions and potential spreading of FUD (fear, uncertainty, and doubt)

  o relevance of the new reframing to a broader group

  o communication channels

It is, basically, a process for the collective inspired by the reframe or idea and driven by the core group that invests most of its time and energy in this venture. Leadership in this phase consists of making sure that all important aspects have been touched, evaluated, and accepted as they are, risks and all.

Choose Your Errors

Fear of losing options by starting to operationalize is a common trap. Leadership means making sure everybody understands that you have to choose your errors collectively. In life only very rarely is there no downside to any choice. Optimizing for one quality will be at the expense of another valuable quality. There is no way to avoid that choice or its consequences. The risk at this stage is that you may to try to avoid choosing, searching for a solution without pain or downside, and, as a result, delaying too long or even worse ending up with a compromise where every quality is mediocre.

Once you're ready to say "this option is enough, choices have been made, when balance in decisions shifts to sufficiency, when 'great' becomes the enemy of the 'good enough'," then it's time to commit.

Engaging Stakeholders

When cultivating social flows, remember that people are involved. We don't mean idealized, composite averages of demographics of people, but actual, identifiable, live, multi-faceted individuals. Get a sense of what they think and feel. We can explore the use of tools for this process—ranging from user stories to other solution-focused, design-thinking methodologies. We can conduct interviews and surveys or build prototypes for the community to engage with. But, whatever approach we use, we begin this process of incorporating people into the design of feedback tools in the Navigating phase and incorporate a bigger group fully in Operationalizing. Whatever process for getting real participant feedback works for the domain, experience proves the value of including the voice of stakeholders in the creation and implementation of social technologies. It is the best way to improve adoption, to get valuable intelligence for adapting the flows.

Formalizing Organizations

Beyond Mintzberg

We have become accustomed to the word "organization" to describe how people cooperate in working towards a common goal. In 1979, Henry Mintzberg wrote _The Structure of Organizations_, referenced by many as the standard work on how to design organizations. He identified 5 archetypes:

➤ *Simple Structure*—small group

➤ *Machine Bureaucracy*—designed as a machine

➤ *Divisional Structure*—collection of machine bureaucracies

➤ *Professional Bureaucracy*—practice groups: the sort of guild system you see in law firms centered around partners

➤ *Adhocracy*—collection of temporary project structures.

Ever since this work was adopted by the MBA programs, the common method of designing organizations has been to fit a structure to a certain requirement, basically to design a form to execute a task. And then insert the staff into the design. If the design is right, stability and efficiency is deemed optimal. If not, you modify the design and/or change the staff. The implied assumption in the description of all these forms is that you design them as if you were an engineer: design them to fit to a certain requirement, to execute a task. And force fit the staff/people into the design.

Again we see the desire for unity and equilibrium, and the quest to engineer a machine to create a desired outcome. In practice, people in these organizations often experience frustration and energy-drains. And the results, then, are sub-optimal.

This frustration has led to experiments with egalitarian organizations, where hierarchy is seen as the enemy. The work of Frederic Laloux shows how the boundary has been shifted, how more and more organizations are shifting away from the stereotypes of Mintzberg. These alternatives have their own issues to deal with.

Organizational Hybrids

Nathaniel James writes for us about the organization of communities in his essay contribution to this project. As a practitioner-strategist of social change, he questions the much-heralded downfall of hierarchical forms of organization, in the wake of the Internet and web revolution. He says that the theory of heterarchical organizations designed for collective action misses the need for some sort of nexus to safeguard organizational coherence, remove internal threats, and form an entry point for financial support. James uses different examples in his essay to show that through some sort of applied (but not controlling) corporatism we can fully pursue the network's real potential. He argues that only by embracing the challenges and contradictions that emerge in community-corporate hybrids can we hope to design social flows that create the change we hope to see.

We also spoke with **Robin Chase,** author of *Peers Inc.* She argues that a community-corporate hybrid organized in the form of peer-production systems is the only form that can match the speed and scale of our society today. The idea has been shown to function in Zipcar and in her newer ventures as well as many others she highlights.

Peer-production systems (think Lyft, Uber, Airbnb as current famous examples) may scale very quickly if the community (people with cars, houses, etc.) can engage the unused capacity of each peer. This capacity exists in the abundance of unused resources that we all have lying around, like a place to sleep, transportation, power tools, and so on. A peer-production system that somehow opens up these resources to others does not need to invest in additional assets and is not bounded by the supply side. Many refer to this as the Sharing Economy. We expect more of these peer-production organizations to look at cooperative structures rather than corporations with a central hub, as they find greater balance between a central-control organization and the community or network sharing it enables.

The key to the scale of network production appears to be switching from social hierarchy to process hierarchy. It isn't about individuals who manage what others do, it is about having processes that we agree to and become accountable to. With functional hierarchy, power corrupts; with process hierarchy there is less ego, there is more purpose.

Organizational Ideas as a Result Instead of a Start

We believe that forms start with people coalescing around a purpose. Cooperation requires solving practical issues like acquiring and allocating resources, agreements on who contributes what, internal and external communication, resolving conflict and dilemmas, and so on. But only to the extent that there are issues that need to be solved: they only need to be "solved" enough to fit the purpose of the entity, the capacity and skills and motivations of the people involved, the entity's size, and what its environment demands. Organizational solutions are to be fitted around the individuals: they are a result, not the starting point.

Using tried and tested concepts and ideas on how to solve these challenges is excellent, if you pick and choose based on merit, fitting to the situation. The other way around (choosing a model and stuffing people in it) is wrong.

Even when we believe many social flows function best in process hierarchy, there is a place for all that has been discovered and tried in the past: parts of functional hierarchies, or for parts of peer production. It depends on what needs to be solved, and for how long.

Solutions are transient: scale makes a lot of difference, people grow, society changes. To grow and extend our reach with our reframe, we have to choose a path or approach to scale.

Scaling Up or Out

When your group is ready to operationalize, you will be collectively clear about the frame and how to navigate it: the way—or ways—you are viewing the situation and the paths through it. The new relationships between people and the new ideas should be enriched with a story that people can coalesce around, understand, own, and expand. The strategy and the scenarios will have been built; the first deliverable will have been identified.

Now it is time for action: for getting results that prove that the narrative works. It is time to let the rubber meet the road: to operationalize. Sure, you have been operating to some degree, but this is about scaling that up or out beyond your small group. It is about creating the form and flows to enable the idea to expand its reach.

We find that several methods are often combined in this phase:

➢ You may start a bigger community or network with a challenge to each other to act. It could be an enduring group or an intentionally temporary one. It may take various shapes as it emerges as a form fitting for growth.

➢ It may help to create or modify the internal processes and governance of the group to achieve the desired effects as it grows.

➢ And finally, information and communication technology can be used to enable social flows, and scale the idea to larger numbers of people, which we will cover at the end of Part Three.

A new idea and a new design may be great, but, for effect, they have to be adopted by enough people to make a difference in the wider world. You have a membrane around the group that holds the idea, and some basic principles for what it means to be inside that membrane. However, you cannot expect everyone else to go through the same process of reframing and navigating as the first group has; you have to operationalize the ideas further, in order to lower the threshold for adoption and get to the intended scale of use. You have to expand to the next level.

The obvious way to scale is to build a hierarchy and expand its size: scaling up means bigger numbers in the same hierarchy. Think of an army, where central command goes "up" by adding people, resources (bigger numbers), and layers beneath it. This is the traditional approach to scaling.

The opposite method is to replicate: growing in scale means spinning out self-organized copies of more or less the same size. Some large enterprises have been built on replication, like the IT-company BSO in the Netherlands founded by the entrepreneur Eckart Wintzen. He designed self-organized units that were split up once their size exceeded 50 people, supported by a small back-office. Many law-firms owned by partners are essentially a conglomerate of units with their own profit-and-loss run by their respective partners, under one brand. Buurtzorg (see below) with thousands of employees consists of small self-organized units. Franchise organizations use this concept, and service clubs like Rotary scale with local chapters.

There is another exciting method to scale, much less known and understood: emergent scaling. At first it may seem like replication, as you can identify multiple independent entities or units that seem to do more or less the same thing. When you dig deeper (or take a helicopter view) you start to see that the relationships and agreements between the units create something that transcends the addition of the parts. The network creates a new function, meaning, strength, and purpose that emerges from the combination of parts and relationships. There is no identifiable hierarchy with a head honcho, yet there is one emergent value. You can identify the emergent property by isolating a unit (breaking the relationships) and seeing what you lose. We use this example more than once in this book, but the Internet is by far the most successful example of emergent scaling (see for more details see the Conclusion on page 207), and one we all know and use. The Internet emerges from the more than 25,000 independent networks that (willingly, although sometimes reluctantly) abide by a basic set of agreements on how data traffic is handled. Isolate one network from the rest of the Internet and its value is lost.

Although the science of emergent scaling is young (starting with Santa Fe Institute, Barabási and others) one thing is sure: relationships between units define whether something can emerge. Relationships require communication, so it's no wonder that Internet and smartphones have accelerated the development of network effects: look at social media, and companies grabbing the benefits of network effects (AirBnB, eBay, Uber, etc.). Are these companies an example of emergent scaling? We hesitate to say so, as they try to own and monetize relationships and network effects. They do use some of the principles, so it is worth studying the underpinnings.

So when considering scale, what is your priority: out (replicated) or up (hierarchical)? Are you aiming for network effects and emergence, exciting but less understood? Here are some guidelines:

Scaling up using hierarchy creates mass and hitting power; it has easy identification (for outsiders) of who handles power, who to deal with. It maintains clear decision-making authority but at the price of becoming inflexible, slow to adapt, and turning the focus inward. It is used for producing a limited range of consistent products or services by taking advantage of efficiencies of scale in production. The best implementations invest heavily in Lean concepts to fight the disadvantages.

Scaling out using replication lowers the threshold for spreading the idea so that more can engage. The tradeoff is that it is more difficult to create mass for impact by coordination. Replicated units tend to grow in different directions and create more diversity, which is great. But it is harder to embed and diffuse what is learned in other units, harder to take new leaps together.

Scaling out is best for location-specific or culture-specific efforts like social enterprises that are not hinged on owning a process but, instead, are tied to expanding an impact. We won't say more about its use for revolutionary purposes ;-).

> Emergent scaling has great potential but it is new and less understood. If you see the need for a network effect, for creating something that emerges out of the cooperation of independent units you should start with studying why the Internet works, how network effects are created in social media, and what scale-free networks are. (_Linked_ by Albert-László Barabási)

The answers to scaling questions will significantly influence governance decisions in the operationalizing stage—decisions about how to create forms. You might even consider unscaling (Peter Vander Auwera describes unscaling based on Amanda Palmer's idea of creating many unique experiences from her onlyness, replicating a quality of experience rather than an identical product or service. Borrowing from Nilofer Merchant's newest work, he describes onlyness as "that thing that only that one individual can bring to a situation. It includes the journey and passions of each human.")

Emergent Scaling in Practice

Networks built on platforms

Some forms tap into network production, using a platform. In the Social Era, these multi-tiered organizations, where the center creates a platform for a network of participants to sell goods and services, can easily outperform organizations that do everything in-house. These are some hub-and-spoke network examples:

> ➢ *Etsy*, the online marketplace for craft people, has a very small central organization. It creates a platform—a marketplace for individual creators (outside the organization) to sell goods effectively.

> ➢ *Bla Bla Car* does car sharing. Car-owning members offer shared rides and share fuel costs with riders. Bla Bla Car depends on a wide network of ride shares, so it focuses its internal structure on supporting that network. A high level of trust and transparency is important for people to interact and share their cars with others. (There is a particular intimacy in being in a car with a stranger.) To win high trust in the network, it employs 70 moderators to ensure interactions are smooth. This is the main factor in making the community-corporation hybrid work. What mattered to its purpose was community, so it created light internal structures to support that. It doesn't own the network, it cares for and feeds it with moderators.

> ➢ *Buurtzorg*, an example referenced before, provides neighborhood care by replicated teams. The network is supported by a platform run by 11 employees, to support 6,000 nurses taking care of patients. The organization starts from the belief that these nurses can give the best care by customizing their service for individual patients. Trusting its nurses to decide how best to care for patients, Buurtzorg asked "what do we need to do to support them?" It settled on lower administration time, coordination, and some minimal structure to keep it together. It dispensed with managers for the nurses. It created a light central form supporting numerous nodes at the edges. Central office doesn't decide what is efficient, the local nurse does. It wanted customization at the edges to serve its purpose, so it selected a network structure.

Decentralized organizations

The network production examples above do have a small, lightweight central platform. It has shifted to being in service to the network, but the platform is still the place where power and wealth can amass. There are many who want to push further into decentralized organizational forms. Officially, these organizations are worker-owned cooperatives. Let's look at two examples: Sensorica and Enspiral. Both have hundreds of participants and processes for getting work done without a functional hierarchy. They use distributed, decentralized approaches to production and have attracted a community of practitioners. Participants may be individuals or organizations. Both have implicit and explicit social benefit agendas.

> ➤ *Sensorica* is an open-source sensor company that produces parts and provides services around gathering data from the physical world. It makes and services sense-making instruments: electronic, mechanical, and optical. Sensorica developed a methodology to open-source 3-D printing and makerspaces activities. In theory its system has no social limitations to scale, whether it has 100 people or 100,000 people, the organization does what it does in the same way; it follows the same processes and procedures including those relating to sales and distribution of funds for everyone. Its main challenge will be finding ways to make it navigable as size increases.

> ➤ *Enspiral* is a network of people and organizations aiming to create a thriving society. Some of the organizations and people code software, others provide education or services. Enspiral focuses on creating high-trust relationships and effective consensus decision-making processes. Its process has evolved into a collaborative decision-making software offering: <u>Loomio</u>. Each Enspiral participant or participating organization makes custom agreements with the Foundation about the percentage of revenue it contributes to health, wellbeing, and maintenance of the Foundation. It has even made process software (for decision-making) to help navigate the complexity of these internal relationships. Specifically, Enspiral has given rise to <u>Cobudget</u>, a way for people to allocate budgets together (more social process software!) Because everything with Enspiral is high-trust and custom agreements, in order to reach extensive scale it must either federate into multiple groups, each of which has high trust within it (scale out/ franchise), or standardize relationships to use a scale-up approach.

If you visit the fringe of decentralized organizations and process hierarchy, you find <u>Decentralized Autonomous Organizations (DAOs)</u> as the dream vision of the blockchain fanatic: entities that run themselves without human involvement. A DAO is like having robots at the center following process hierarchies, with humans assigned tasks at the organization's edges. It doesn't need social protocols except where it interacts with humans. (**Arthur Brock** writes about <u>Sovereign Accountable Commons</u>—a more humane version.)

However scaling is approached, we still need forms and flows to know how to interact, have clear expectations of each other, and be productive together.

The Facets of Operationalizing

In the coming chapters, we will first explore *forms*, then *flows* before looking at the *information technologies* that can support the social flows we are cultivating.

We achieve *forms* to operate with by starting (or revising existing) communities, networks, corporations, and other forms of collective action. The traditional focus of organizational design is on the inside of an entity: how to design functions, how to make the gears mesh, who does what, who decides. Our focus is on embedding the community or group in the societal flow: what shape of form and permeability of membrane is needed to engage with the flow and to influence it? To be embedded means to be influenced by, as well as to influence, what is around us. So what is needed to make that happen, what is needed to have a dialog, to engage, and to respond? We see that the most successful forms start with identifying what is on the outside that they need to interact with and then working their way back into finding the form that best suits their external purpose. The relationships on the inside of the organizational membrane need to be just sufficient to support the activities of engaging outside that membrane.

Rather than an exhaustive list of possible forms, we offer in Chapter 5 a few more recent forms, which are best suited to social flows.

Flows are the subject of Chapter 6. Flows are connections and agreements on how to achieve goals together both within and between forms, at scale. This is all about how the inside of the entity supports the scaling up and/or out. A couple of people can come up with ways to get things done together, but as the number of people involved increases, the amount of time negotiating with each other can also increase exponentially.

By having some agreements on standardized interactions and standardized processes for repeating actions, we can focus on the work instead of how we will get it done.

Coherence plays a significant role as we scale up, challenging us in the stairstep jumps of social dynamics as we grow and expand. We increase our need for agreements between our entity and within it. Governance (one of the three core aspects of Coherence) is about how to create and change agreements, how to modify (or even eliminate) those processes. Governance exists at each level of emergence of entities. Remember, we used to call this management, but we want to distinguish between top-down organization and self-regulating collectives, so we have used governance to describe this.

In the Introduction we showed that we see these not as an engineer designing a machine, but as a biochemist looking at the process hierarchy of life. Social technology should support entities (groups) with membranes (inside-outside), and flows through the membranes between the entities. Social technology should also enable ensembles of entities to emerge. Ensembles will start to act as a new, bigger entity with its own membrane of coherence. And so on.

In Chapter 7—the last chapter of Part Three—we focus on a specific domain of practice for social flows. We look at how *physical or information technology* can enhance social flows. Throughout history humans have adopted new technology which allows us to bypass our physical and mental limits: faster, higher, bigger, smaller, deeper, longer, larger, farther. We may often not notice it, but physical technology can also spur innovations in social technology, supporting new ideas. Be it money represented by bits so it can flow fast as light, or hashtags on Twitter to organize subjects in a river of information, or radical customization of services at low cost.

Here perhaps is our greatest opportunity to leverage information technology in support of social flows to reach scales previously unthinkable. To do so well, will demand a strong understanding of how physical and information technology creates conditions for better social flows.

Again, designing physical or information technology for process hierarchies requires a different mindset than is usually taught at traditional schools.

Quick Guide to Operationalizing

Form and Flow Drive Operationalization

Social technology differs from physical technology in that it doesn't follow strict laws, it is not perfectly replicable, it is human-centric, and functions as a learning system.

We use the terms "forms" and "flows" to evoke the biological and emergent qualities of social flows, rather than words like "structure" and "management."

Triggers to Operationalize

➢ the new reframing has been increased in strength by exploring it (as opposed to being weakened, with more doubts added)

➢ risks are understood clearly enough, and the first deliverable and sufficient resources are in place

➢ some sense of contingency plan and immune system is also in place

Choose Your Errors

Optimizing for one quality will be at the expense of another valuable quality. There is no way to avoid that choice or its consequences. The risk is that you may to try to avoid choosing, searching for an imagined solution that is without pain or downside.

Engage Stakeholders

Participant feedback works and experience proves the value of including the voice of stakeholders in the creation and implementation of flow and form:

➢ Consider alternative forms to the typical ones described by Mintzberg.

- Combine and weave together forms, using the strengths of each to compensate for the weaknesses of the other to create organizational hybrids, such as those that engage people in peer production.

Forms start with people coalescing around a purpose, not with a blueprint. The organizational solutions are to be fitted around the purpose and individuals.

Scale

> ➤ Traditional scaling involves expanding a hierarchy, adding numbers and layers. We can also expand our reach by replicating: building similar units. Most recently we have started to explore emergent scaling, where network effects create an emergent property of the whole. Platforms that provide for peer production are a step in that direction.

CHAPTER 5:

FORMS FOR SOCIAL FLOWS

Forms to Help People to Cooperate

A huge question in implementing and shaping a social flow is what form the social engagement happens in. In the introduction to Part Three, we defined a form by focusing on the boundary of an entity and the interactions with its environment that create cooperation. Its shape is also driven by its internals, the set of most important agreements we make that create the cooperation of the internals of the membrane.

Agreements can manifest themselves in various guises, can carry different names, and have different properties. In common language, we use names like ritual, behavior, rules, contracts, regulations, and so on. The commonality is that there is a basic agreement, even a philosophy of sorts, on how to interact and cooperate.

When we talk about form, some people focus on the legal agreement concerning how a collective is organized. Legal structures which mitigate risk are useful and should be designed and used to support these social cooperation agreements—but, here, we will not be concerned with legal structures: a lawyer can help take these agreements and express them in terms of legal structure, if necessary. Legal agreements are hardly the only or the strongest type of agreement in practice. Verbal unwritten agreements (the bond of a "band of brothers") can be more binding and powerful than legal written agreements, for example. A closely knit group can ignore traditional legal structures: the core of experts in a particular field often feel more allegiance to their peers than to their respective employers. The reverse is also true: a formal membership does not mean you'll be accepted in the "inner circle." So if legal structures and formal memberships do not define boundaries, what does?

Being Inside or Outside

Any affiliation of people will develop a boundary or threshold that has to be crossed to be inside of its "membrane." Most people have an innate sense of being "inside" or "outside" this boundary. They attach an identity to the collective "inside."

The repressive manifestation of this tendency is when cohesion is imposed on people, when rituals and observable behavior are codified and enforced. The benign version is when there is a self-generated coherence between individuals, when the purpose is shared within a diverse group. We focus here on how to achieve coherence by sharing a purpose.

What are the qualities of that identifier that implicitly define the boundary? The more obvious qualities are clear. For network behavior like the hashtag, inclusion is simply the act of using the hashtag. For membership organizations there may be lengthy criteria. For a corporation, to be inside it, you have to be hired. The way that boundary functions is a core element of that particular form and the liquefaction of this membrane is a key part of what <u>Nilofer Merchant</u> described in <u>*11 Rules for Creating Value in the #SocialEra*</u>. Even traditional organizations are learning how to be more open and put more gradation in the spectrum of activity between the inside and outside of the organization.

Human nature strives however for a deeper and less explicit form of belonging.

Human Drive to Belong—to be Inside

The drive to "belong" to a group, to an affiliation, is very strong. A lot of research is now available showing how the higher brain functions in babies develop in their first 9-12 months. At birth only the brainstem and very primary functions are developed. <u>Alan Schore</u> describes how the cortex and prefrontal cortex grow and form by close empathic interactions with their primary attachment figure, usually the mother. A sense of self-confidence and the capacity for empathy are formed in this first year. Safe attachment to the parents builds the capacity (and need) to exist in safe social groups, groups where members "lift each other up." Evolutionarily this capacity and this need to belong makes a lot of sense: groups have a better chance of survival than individuals.

Being inside makes someone who is empathic feel co-responsible (together with the rest of the group) for safety, security, and caring: the prerequisites for a healthy environment.

> ➢ Safety is about defense: preventing external and internal attacks that threaten the existence of the group, maintaining an active immune system that adapts, learns, and acts.

➤ Security is about resources and resilience. A group of people must be able to shift burdens when needed, to lend support, resources, and strength to each other, so their network is stronger than the sum of its parts.

➤ Care is about allowing each other to take chances, about resolving conflict and dilemmas, about collective and individual learning from mistakes, helping each other up when we fall down.

A group must be able to create safety, security, and care for each other, otherwise it is not felt to be a functional group. People who do not act co-responsible are ejected, if only informally. People who act co-responsible but are not part of the formal structure for a group are nonetheless incorporated. If formal memberships and legal structures do not align with this need, or even conflict with it, the natural social flow is disrupted. This creates stress and anxiety. Bypasses are sought, alternatives created.

The boundaries to look for are these natural "inside-outside" definitions. Formal and legal structures fit best when they align with the natural boundaries. At a minimum they should not be an interference or a block.

Safety, security and care are prerequisites, but not the driving force. Purpose is.

Purpose

When we no longer treat people as hired cogs in the machine of our entities and no longer use hierarchy to force them to cooperate, then more compelling reasons are needed for people to engage productively in an entity. Purpose solves this. Form does not create purpose but purpose will drive form. And in most cases, purpose is directed at making an impact in your environment. Purpose creates intent.

Forms do not follow the laws of gravity. Forms aren't made of wood, glass, or silicon. They are constructed by relationships and agreements between people, people who share energy, attention, resources, and wisdom and who are working toward a common purpose. Having a clear aspiration, a purpose, a "why" in the shared rich narrative often unites a collective more than agreement on "how." People who share the narrative tend to be aspirational, passionate, and resourceful about it. They will find and invent solutions where necessary and they only need enough form to allow them to follow their passion.

Like we said in the introduction to Part Three, when it comes to organizational structures, do not try to fix anything that is not broken simply because the archetype of the structure demands it. The form of an entity needs to support that passion and creativity while handling conflicts and dilemmas. Goals and key principles for behavior arise from clear purpose.

Goals

With clear purpose, we saw in our research that people themselves often facilitated the development of group goals. For example, **Edgeryders** has a broad general purpose of "solving the global societal, economic, environmental, security and energy problems threatening Europe and humanity in general." The specific projects and goals they develop as a collective emerge through group events or client opportunities. (One such effort is their Unmonastery, which is a lightweight format for enabling people to contribute their skills and ideas to a local community in exchange for basics like housing and food.) Productivity is purpose-driven at Edgeryders, and it keeps its form light and agile.

To Engage Passion, Use Participatory Patterns

We notice participatory patterns for conversations are emerging just ahead of this cultivating social flows work. Human understanding of patterns for group participation is now sophisticated enough that we can be very time efficient in achieving our collective goals together. _The Surprising Power of Liberating Structures_ by Henri Lipmanowicz and Keith McCandless offers a set of over 30 patterns that can support groups in clarifying and achieving their purpose. These patterns are structures and processes for having productive conversations in groups ranging from three to thousands of members. We are evolving more patterns to be responsive, agile, and adaptive to our needs and purpose. We saw many of our practitioners using these patterns (and others) to achieve high engagement and productivity with groups toward their purpose and goals, especially when they wanted to bring in stakeholders.

Key Behavior Principles

We also saw that social flow endeavors encouraged the definition of the key principles for community behavior and expectations aligned with that purpose, so people know what behavior is appropriate, both inside the form and outside it. These might be encapsulated into little sayings like "the wiki way" which means you make errors easy to fix rather than hard to make. These key principles set the structure for behavior, what is acceptable and what is not, creating the shape of behavior and action for the flow. The key principles are the ways in which behavior can embody the values that the group holds. When people new to the group are clear about the purpose and goals, as well as the key principles, they can decide whether to join, work with, or partner with the entity or not. The entity can then attract appropriate participants.

Un-Tayloring

Growing our form also requires us to understand and select how we will be productive together and how we will define productivity. This may be implicit in our overall design, and here is the chance to be explicit about it. If we are spreading an idea or meme, productivity may look like the rate of uptake of the meme or instances of the idea. And the activity of nurturing the use of the idea may seem random or emergent rather than controlled and directed. If ours is an organization that produces tangible goods, then productivity looks quite different: something like being able to meet demand at an acceptable cost.

Ton van Asseldonk points out that to be productive in delivering goods and services you have to be able to match the complexity of your environment. Industrialization in the 20th century with Taylorist management and assembly lines created high productivity and thus low cost per unit, as long as the demand was for (cheap) mass-produced, identical units. Production was fit for low-complexity demands from the environment.

The same structure is extremely unproductive and expensive if the demand is for highly customized products and services: high complexity. In service organizations the same effect can be seen: the inflexibility of Taylorist service organizations is best described by the hell called a "customer service call-center." This is a low-complexity offering facing a high-complexity environment.

The so-called Lean Production methods—inspired by the Toyota Production System—that have arisen are all about un-Tayloring production organizations, so they can meet the fickle demand for custom products and services. An adaption for more complex environments, un-Tayloring turns Taylorist management on its head:

> ➤ The most valuable resource is the experience and know-how of people on the shop floor, which is increased and used as much as possible.

> ➤ There is no assembly line, but instead parallel processing in units that do as many steps as possible and are highly flexible in what they produce, made possible by intelligent people on the shop floor.

> ➤ The best planning is no planning, meaning being fast enough to be able to respond to demands instead of needing to predict them.

This has proven highly effective in both production and services. Unfortunately, many schools still teach Taylorist approaches and not simply as history.

Forms Grow and People Change

Forms are anything but static as the collective grows.

Every time the size of a group or a process grows by 200% or more, it is like entering a new landscape: a form that works at a smaller scale may fail spectacularly when the size passes a new threshold. As people join in and become participants, the need arises to create forms to enable the network to flow. Knowledge, decisions, and actions need to continue to flow as we scale up or out. There is a dance between keeping it highly customized to the individuals present and the standardization that provides consistency across the effort, so we appear as a unified whole.

In *Reinventing Organizations*, Frederic Laloux shows how, over time, more sophisticated forms have been developed to cope with changing demands: not only the demands of the task at hand, but the needs of those joining the structure to be valued and challenged, and to exert influence on the collective. Intelligent, educated, socially-sensitive people hate to spend their time doing stupid, repetitive tasks because someone else tells them to; they desire much more in return for their time and energy. The evolution of forms may very well be driven more by the desire of those joining the collective wanting to get more out of their time than anything else.

Moving away from hierarchies, where decisions are made by superiors and tasks accomplished by their inferiors, is not just an effort to get more social engagement. The challenge is deeper than a shift in structure and this is part of why we are writing this book. Cultivating social flows is not a simple hack on form... or we could end up with the tyranny of structurelessness or other errors. It is about designing for humans, as we are, to leverage our strengths and achieve things together... even in (or because of) the complexity of our society.

As we design for agility and adaptive capacity, rigid forms turn out to be brittle over time. People and their intentions shift (even if the organization does not), the rigid form does not exploit the potential of the collective intelligence in matching a changing environment. Rigid forms tend to turn inward and into power struggles. One of the many benefits of forms that support emergent process hierarchies instead of functional hierarchies, for example, is that they reduce the abuse of positional power where superiors retort, "because I said so".

Embedding in Your Environment

Amsterdam is a city of cyclists. Everywhere you see old and young on a bicycle. Parents bring their kids to school in a specially designed sleek cargo bicycle, while older students weave through traffic on older machines. Every day, over half a million bicycle trips are made in the city. There are as many bicycles in the city as inhabitants (800,000).

Cyclists act like they are kings of the road, often ignoring red signals. Nobody wears a helmet, but you are 50 times less likely to be involved in a serious accident on a bicycle than in New York City. Car drivers are used to the cyclists and make allowances. The massive parking lots near train stations hold literally thousands of bikes and attract tourists to take pictures.

The Dutch are fond of cycling to start with, but the popularity of cycling in Amsterdam has been stimulated by a deliberate attempt to involve the community of cyclists over a long period. Michael van der Vlist, Alderman of Amsterdam (1978-1990), decided to let local cyclists tell the city how to improve cycling conditions. He extended the membrane of who was included on the inside of developing the design. He included the stakeholders who were experiencing it.

The rising popularity of owning and driving a car had led to crowded and unsafe roads. He reasoned that bicyclists, as daily users, would have an excellent idea of what irritated them, what was dangerous and what was safe, what shortcuts would reduce journey times, which the popular routes were, and how to stay away from car traffic. He arranged for an existing community of cyclists to be the spokespeople for all cyclists. His civil servants would add their expertise on what they could afford, execution issues, and long-term planning versus short-term fixes. The cyclist would lead on priorities.

After a slow start of getting used to each other, the arrangement started to bring results, mostly quick fixes. After 5-10 years, the long-term planning effects became visible. And now you can find wonderful safe and fast lanes for cyclists crossing the city, often perpendicular to heavy car traffic flows, or separated from the other traffic lanes. In Amsterdam, you can often travel faster by bicycle than by car, with the additional benefit of having no parking problems or parking costs. (The only drawback is that bicycles get stolen more often.) Continuous investment is made to keep up with the growth in cycle use. No wonder cycling is popular!

The word "inclusion" is widely used in current jargon. While on the surface that seems like it means opening the doors wide, what it means in practice is being more mindful about what those doors look like and who is implicitly being invited through them or turned away. In practice, we are defined as much by what we include as what we exclude.

Once we are clear on the qualities of our boundaries, we have to explore how we want to interact with what is outside whatever we call the boundaries. For something like hashtags and a network, there is no control or collective action, only emergent action from the parts. For an organization, whether corporation or for-benefit organization, the questions can be lengthy and complex. The key issues are how to get inter-organizational collaboration and how your dialogue with your ecosystem influences your internal design.

Recursiveness and Flow

The biological metaphor helps us again. A cell is an entity, forming an organ by cooperating with other more or less similar cells; organs cooperate to form a living being, with a skin, which breathes and eats and excretes. Each emergent level creates more richness, but holds the same principles. The thoughts on how to interact within an entity, within a boundary, can be transcended to the next emergent level. At that level entities interact with each other, and create a common boundary that defines inside and outside. Like 25,000 networks that create the Internet together: the Internet is very real, very defined but an emergent property of its parts.

Humans can feel themselves to be part of many entities at the same time. Part of a family, a neighborhood, a company, a sports team, a group of friends who go fishing, a political movement, a church, a nation. Each entity has its own purpose and its own form, and may be embedded in a bigger emergent entity. We humans have no problem with this multitude of overlapping and multi-level emergent entities; we switch easily between these allegiances and their identities. A switch brings up the sense of how our core entity is embedded in bigger ensembles, and up again. People who are seen as "good at politics" have a good sense of the interactions and thus flows between entities and between emergent levels.

Flow is about the interaction with the environment needed both to survive (bills have to be paid, people come and go) and to contribute to a bigger shared purpose, to influence the environment. Agreements have to be made on who does what, what resources are contributed or exchanged, and how information is shared, decisions are made, immune systems are set up, conflicts are resolved and so on. We will cover more on these agreements in the coherence section of the next chapter.

Permeability Works Both Ways

The **Edgeryders** example shows that a boundary is a membrane which is permeable: you influence your outside, but the reverse is also true. And sometimes the outside is toxic to you....

Edgeryders started out as an online community. Collaborating on the web led them naturally to decentralization. People were holding many conversations at the same time. Some of these conversations led to action. The rule that emerged was this: whoever wanted action was responsible for taking the first step and leading. Edgeryders ended up drawing legitimacy from action, and that made them a do-ocracy. A mantra started to circulate: "Who does the work, calls the shots."

It turned out that organizations wanted to work with them. The only way to do this was to build a company on top of the online community, a company that could act as interface. So they did. They thought they could do it without changing their way of working. In fact, they badly wanted not to change it.

This is how they did it: some people from the community had experience in business and finance. They were to be the "money guys" who would keep track of legal issues and finance. The Edgeryders community let them choose the jurisdiction they were most comfortable with (they chose the UK) and asked them to incorporate. Edgeryders just saw the legalities and procedures involved with running a company as boxes to tick, and they ticked them. Then they went back to work.

This turned out to be a mistake. Information was hoarded and decisions became hard to make without the information. Hard and costly lessons learnt, a year later they evolved principles to adhere to, solving this issue. They increased transparency by:

> ➤ using the cloud, so information was visible

> ➤ keeping it simple—bare bones

> ➤ sharing responsibility

> ➤ not cutting corners

> ➤ keeping a written record

Edgeryders claims, "Every time you don't make the effort to share a piece of information, you are hoarding knowledge and power."

Immune System

The example shows the need to be aware that interactions are necessary but not without risk. An immune system can protect your entity up to a point from bad actors or attacks. Reserves of money and resources do help, removal of bad actors should be quick, but these actions are obvious. We observed other strategies that mobilized resources from other entities and powers.

If you develop many fans who feel that they will benefit from your existence (be it mutuality of protection, or making life easier), they can be brought into action when needed. You see groups spending a lot of energy on creating these fans.

In Amsterdam when the Municipality started the Fiber-to-the-Home project, the opposition from cable companies was intended to create uncertainty and doubt by spinning stories, trying to undermine political support for the project. The project group countered that approach by developing a wide network of experts worldwide, nicknamed "Friends-Of-Fiber." These experts voluntarily contributed counterarguments with publicly available sources to the project group. The information was publicized immediately after a story emerged, in a brutally honest manner: if a story was true, it was acknowledged to be true. The honesty and availability of independent fact-checking sources contributed over time to the project's reputation for being sound and dependable. That reduced the effect of new spins.

Sharing intelligence on what is happening in your environment continuously in a core group, as big as possible, builds both better intelligence to see something coming, and also creates, to the outside, a sense of unity: "You cannot play these guys against each other."

Some people have a natural tendency for diplomacy and building bridges and relationships, but find it hard to deal with attacks. Others know how to fight and do not mind if relationships are damaged, if necessary, but grow tired of diplomacy. Knowing and acknowledging each other's strengths, and consciously applying these strengths to the situation, creates a strong immune system for the group.

Matching the Complexity of Your Environment

Ton van Asseldonk has developed a rigorous, formal mathematical definition of the complexity of an organization. Complexity is defined as the richness of responses to demands. Low complexity means a limited number of responses, while high complexity means a large variety of responses.

He maps the organization to a network and measures two things:

1. the number of relationships in the network divided by the number of nodes (connectivity)
2. how the relationships are distributed (centralization)

The combination is a measure of complexity. Low complexity is the tell-tale of a centralized network with a limited number of relationships; high complexity indicates the opposite.

Complexity comes at a cost: more and more energy and attention is needed to keep the network stable and find the right response for the demand, and more and more initiative and self-steering is demanded of the people who form the network.

His theory says that you only need the complexity that is demanded of you by your environment: having much more is costly and less productive. He has tested the theory by analyzing soccer games. All 11 players in a team were mapped as nodes in a network, and passing the ball to each other showed the relationships between the nodes. When full games of 2 x 45 minutes were measured in this way, the numbers proved that the winning team nearly always showed a little more complexity than the losing opponent!

The key lesson is that embedding in your environment dictates the number of relationships, the variety of responses, and therefore the internal complexity.

Evolving a Form

Our learning is that no single form is always right; rather, each form type has a right place and time, has to match the context as well as people and their motives. Each has a sort of lifespan or evolutionary position in a sequence.

It is tempting to design a form that you, in your mind, think suits everyone. That is a trap. In practice, the best forms evolve out of the collective, out of the development of the common understanding, out of practice and issues that need to be solved in the ecosystem. It is a great help and accelerator if knowledge and wisdom is available about possible forms, about processes, and about governance, if lessons from others can be learned and used. Yet the application should be a group process where everybody learns and contributes.

We scanned our research and experience to create this list of questions to consider:

➢ Did we start with a clean slate or with a template we were taught or used before? Is that template a conscious choice or a coincidence?

➢ What is the purpose of the form, what problem needs to be solved that arises from the lack of structure or process? If there is no problem, don't fix it.

➢ What decisions are made where, by whom? How are conflicts or dilemmas resolved?

➢ How are decisions reached?

➢ How does the collective interact with what is outside of it?

- the state
- other producers
- the audience or clients

➢ How volatile is the outside? And do you need to follow that volatility?

➢ How is defense or an immune system against attacks organized?

➢ How is productivity accomplished inside of it?

➢ If there is money or alternative currencies, who controls them?

➢ What enables the new team to stand shoulder to shoulder, both to defend against critics or deniers or other resistance as well as to support each other in the work? What is the WHY that connects them with each other? How do they know they can count on each other? Can they provide security, resources, and care to each other?

➢ How strong is the network? If you don't have one, then work to create one and weave it more tightly and densely.

➢ If your organization is part of an existing larger org. structure, does that larger org. grant enough autonomy, agency, authority, and resources to the team? You might want to pull together a mix of people with social authority (so they can sway others beyond the org. chart), positional authority (so the organization takes them seriously), and attitude for innovation (to foster creativity and curiosity in the group) to achieve this. The larger organization needs to grant the group enough resources and overhead to do their innovation.

The questions are a guideline to reflect on past choices or future proposals.

Life Cycle

If you can create a form and it grows, can it also wither away with age?

The core competence of Connekt (a foundation in the Netherlands that Herman works with) is the creation of forms to engage with a specific societal challenge. For instance, the Dutch Government asked whether better packaging of products for transport could increase the load factor of trucks and, as a consequence, reduce the emissions generated by transporting goods. Less air that has no value and more densely packed products seems great for everyone, but nobody is "in control."

Many parties play a role in this, and each has its own priorities: designing attractive products, creative design of product packaging to support marketing, prevention of damage in transport, reducing the cost of production or the cost of transport, easy handling, recycling or dumping of the packaging, and so on. The approach that Connekt takes is directly aimed at identifying people from all stakeholders who think this is an interesting question and seem willing to think about finding a different approach. The second step is analyzing what natural groups and networks (of people and companies) already exist, for instance around e-commerce and packaging of these products. And, thirdly, which sub-network best meets the preconditions for starting a form (energy of people for the subject, potential for improvement, importance of taking a step for players). The best fitting sub-network is invited to a kick-off meeting where the narrative is explained and tested, including identifying next steps. If the preparation work is done well, a (sub-)group will coalesce around the goal: let's take a step. Nurturing that group may lead to the creation of a boundary, a shared identity, a shared purpose and goals to achieve, next step to take. The startup, the analysis, and the nurturing is financed by the government; the rest is effort from the entity.

The lifecycle of a form also includes an end, although sometimes a prolonged one. Forms may outlive their purpose and continue to exist as zombies: the legal structure shores up an organization whose goal has become more and more to continue its own existence. As long as there are resources available they continue to exist, sometimes to the detriment of the next form that should take its place.

Cautionary Tales

One particular challenge that arises when using social forms is that none of them ever seems quite right. Whether it is because organizations change over time or because the individuals within them do, the social forms never seem to fit all the time. So as edge practitioners of social flow, we end up having to decide whether to *buy one off the rack or to design one to fit*, so to speak. Many of the practitioners whom we interviewed and heard from use off-the-shelf structures to achieve their goals of social flow. For example, LCL is not innovating on the form of their organization. A few others build new structures from scratch, such as Edgeryders and HolacracyOne (which sells that pattern of structure as a service).

The challenge with making your own custom form is the time it takes to generate, test, refine, and get it functional. A lot of time may end up going to explaining the boundaries, why they were chosen, and how to operate in the form—time that could be spent on being productive on your purpose. The initial time costs can be huge and the risks largely unknown. However, the opportunity for deep bonding in the process of co-creating and achieving fit-to-purpose forms can be compelling. The trouble with using an existing social structure, while it can be quick and easy, is that it may not fit quite right. Even Holacracy, which purposefully allows for shifts in the structure over the lifespan, also takes administrative time and energy to create and manage. For those of us who want to focus on being productive, tinkering with and evolving forms feels like a drag on productivity.

Social forms help us interact by helping us understand who, what, where, when, and how for the group. However, if we have to attend to the form all the time, then our attention is on our own how and not on what we want to achieve. We are still, as a society, figuring out the balance of being emergent and evolutionary in our forms while directing our attention to our tasks.

Forms for Social Flow: Conclusion

What we found in our exploration is that a clear aspiration and purpose—a clear "why"—often unites a collective. We saw that people often facilitated the development of group goals. And they encouraged the definition of the key principle of community behavior and expectations, so people knew how

and what to do. Factors that seemed to help groups excel include not only being clear about who or what is included, but also being clear about what is excluded—or outside the group or the structure. The design needs to engage members to contribute to the issue while growing themselves, and the Social Startup Labs and Skill Camps of LCL show that even in the most deprived urban areas this is possible.

Having decided what is inside and what is outside raises the next issue: how to get inter-organizational collaboration, and how your dialogue with your ecosystem influences your internal design. Being aware of what is important in the dialogue, and matching the complexity inside to the complexity outside, are the key design targets.

What have you discovered in your practice around organizational structures? Share with us and others at CultivatingFlows.com.

Quick Guide to Forms

Forms for Social Flows

Purpose leads to the shape and agreements of the collective which generates the form that an organization takes. The legal structure should support that form and reduce risk for the form.

Inside or Outside

Design the inside structure for the purpose outside of the structure and the environment: just enough form and no more.

> ➤ Organizations create a sense of belonging (whether internally or for fans of a brand), which humans are deeply driven to want.

> ➤ Healthy environments provide safety (defense from attacks), security (resources and resilience), and care (mutual support).

> ➤ Consider how to make the membrane permeable to engage broader participation and stakeholder involvement.

> ➤ Your "membrane" defines both what is inside and outside, and what flow is permitted through the membrane. The latter is as important as the former.

Provide a clear and compelling purpose.

> ➤ Goals arise from that clear purpose.

> ➤ Engage passion rather than imposing structure. Use liberating structures for conversation patterns that are efficient and effective.

Participatory Process

A sense of participation in decision-making engages people's passion, so use conversation patterns that increase participation.

Key Behaviors

Having clear key behaviors or community agreements increases trust and clues participants in to what is expected.

Un-Tayloring

The old model used Taylorist management—highly mechanical. For high customization in complex conditions, we need to un-Taylor production using methods such as Lean Production. The complexity of the form needs to be just sufficient for the complexity of the environment.

Embedding in your Environment

➤ Being inside makes someone responsible (together with the group) for safety, security, and caring: the prerequisites for a healthy environment. If they do not contribute to these factors, they should be outside. Your "immune system" must be able to deal with that.

➤ Your form's internal richness/complexity should match the complexity of the environment. Too little and you adapt too slowly; too much and you waste energy keeping the structure together.

Evolving

Forms evolve and they do so to fit humans. Design forms for humans as we really are and given them a capacity to evolve over time to continue to fit the people within them and their stakeholders.

➤ As with all design, choose your errors and avoid perfectionism. Ask these questions about your organization and its form:
  - new or old?
  - purpose?
  - what problem does it solve?
  - what is the decision-making and conflict-resolution process?
  - immune system?
  - productivity process?
  - who has what authority?
  - how is care, safety, and security provided?
  - autonomy?

Cautionary Tales

Social structures require us to choose our errors: either work with something off-the-shelf with a few custom modifications then focus elsewhere, or take the time and attention to sculpt from scratch.

Chapter 6:

Flows and Coherence

Now that we have explored forms—the shape of the boundaries of an entity and how it interacts with what is outside of it—let's look at the flows within, including the governance of it all. Within flows we see three main types of agreements about action, which we call process protocols, decision-making, and governance.

> ➤ Protocols are "challenge-response" agreements: "if I say this, then you know what types of responses are expected and what these responses will mean to me." Protocols create safety and predictability, even between strangers, because we like to know what to do, what is expected.
>
>   • Within process we sometimes use incentives to make flows visible.
>
> ➤ Clear decision-making process is crucial for entities, so they can deal with conflicts and dilemmas productively.
>
> ➤ Governance is how you are collectively able to adapt, test, and modify behaviors and accountability, and how to deal with exceptions and disasters.

While all of these play a role in coherence, we will specifically focus on coherence through governance in this chapter.

Social Protocols

The predictable and learned patterns of social interactions tend to become invisible through habitual use. We are taught to use them all the time, over and over, to the point where it becomes second nature and we don't realize we are following a routine process and certainly don't question it.

Think about how you have used a phone over the course of your life. Even in the '70s some of us used phones that were on party lines. There were processes for checking if anyone was on the line before dialing. In many families, it was standard to answer the phone with "Hello, *family name* residence." Calling was rare and precious. If the phone rang, you answered it.

Then we developed touch-tone phones instead of rotary. Without party lines, we no longer needed the process of checking to see whether anyone else was on the line. There was a much bigger shift in social protocol when we moved on to wireless phones, taking the phones with us as we moved through our own spaces. We no longer stopped everything to talk. We brought our phones with us into our activities. We shifted process again when we developed answering machines, such as not answering every call that came through, but waiting to hear who was calling before picking up. Then came cell phones, where we developed new social protocols around talking on the phone while driving and while in public. Smartphones have brought new challenges with them and require yet more, new social protocols.

And now, tied to all our different forms of communication, we have meta social process about selecting which channel we are available on, when, and for what. Some might use the message text on Skype to say: "ping me before you call." Or email messages may indicate how an individual prefers to be contacted. Some people hack their out-of-office auto-reply. Mostly, we haven't standardized the social protocols around all these new technologies, so there is a much greater sense that we are bumping up against each other's preferences and comfort zones. We don't yet have a process guide.

Emily Post's *Book of Etiquette* emerged when cities saw a huge influx of residents and people needed to know how to interact. We get anxious if we don't know what the social processes are. We may choose not to follow them, but not knowing stops many people from even participating.

When norms don't emerge or get clarified by a book like Emily Post's, we can end up legislating behaviors. Some companies are even moving from social process to governance policy to regulate the communication challenge, dictating when emails can or can't be sent, for example.

We have social protocols associated with getting on an elevator, opening a meeting, or running a conference, for instance. Social protocols are the steps that we take in doing something, or being something, or having something. They cover the expectation we have of how someone will respond when we say, "Hello. How are you?" We walk into a building together and there are social processes about who opens the door, who goes first through the door, and what is said. Navigating doors tends to be an unspoken process. Social protocol extends to traffic. Flashing your headlights—to indicate to a big rig driver that you will allow him to fall safely in line before you—is not a law but social protocol.

Many social protocols become habits we don't think about—part of what is considered culture. Many clashes between cultures start with someone unwittingly violating a social process of the other side. When you introduce a new social protocol, be aware of the unconscious ones already there.

Humor

We spoke with **Deanna Zandt**, author of _Share This! How You Will Change the World with Social Networking_, about the power of humor and her work in social media and social change endeavors. When we then discussed it with the Flows community, it sparked significant debate. Humor can be an accelerator of connection and lubricant during mediation as well as a source of sensed friction, revealing where people are tense. Humor is both the key indicator of common ground in morals, and the lubricator in relationships.

A lot of humor is based on exposing and tickling taken-for-granted social protocols. As Benjamin Ellis, founding director at SocialOptic, pointed out in our community conversations, you can even use humor to investigate the gap in social protocols. In a merger described by Ellis, two formerly separate groups of people needed to start cooperating and integrating into one. Anyone with experience will tell you that frictions and tensions will start brewing, possibly exploding in your face after some time. The question was, can you detect beforehand if there is little or a lot of difference in the culture of the groups? The answer was provided by humor.

In this example, both groups were brought together in one room. A carefully prepared stand-up comedian started to entertain them, testing the limits of their work culture, what was taboo and what was not in their processes. The observers in the room looked for differences between the groups. When one group did not think something was funny and the other one did, they knew where potential conflicts could arise.

Watch for humor as one possible indicator of coherence, as well as a possible intervention for improving it.

Social Process Lessons from Game Design

To get a grasp of how to see and then adjust social processes, we looked at game design. **Daniel Mezick**, author of _The Culture Game: Tools for the Agile Manager_, defines 'social protocols' as structured interactions between two or more people. They are personal interaction mechanics, lowering the risk of unwittingly violating someone else's space.

What makes a game into a game?

> ➤ you know your role

> ➤ you opt-in

> ➤ there is a clear goal

> ➤ there is a clear rule-set

> ➤ there is a clear way to track progress during the interaction

Similarly, social processes often make clear what your role is (in sharing a meal with others, are you the senior or leader of the group or is it all equals?). You can choose to play or opt out (ask for a check just for your own meal, if you don't want to play the game with others). The goal of a shared meal, bill-splitting process is to ease the tension of conversation over who pays. There is a clear rule set, in the dinner bill conversation it is usually the senior person or leader. During the meal there are smaller social cues triggered by the server about who orders, who checks the wine, etc.

Suppose you decide to go to an event where you hardly know anyone. Once there, you approach someone at the food and drink area, say hello and make small talk, while the other person chooses whether to chat in reply. Once you have both danced through these few steps, someone will branch off in the conversation or both parties can walk away to other areas. The roles are those of greeter and responder. It is optional for both parties. There are steps that both have some sense of, although the details are specific to the situation. The goal is to see if you want to continue talking or move on.

In software development, <u>Agile Methodologies</u> has brought in a series of processes around <u>Standup meetings</u>. The goal is to keep everyone aware of what everyone else is doing and solve any challenges people have. They are called Standup meetings because people literally stand up, which helps limit the meeting to 15 minutes. Everyone participating knows the procedure and gives an update on what they've been doing and what their goal is for the day, along with any challenges they anticipate. Everyone can see if the processes are being followed: stand, say what you've been doing, what needs to be done, and where you need help.

Processes are a good, satisfying way to game your interactions. The game element can be used for meeting strangers safely, but can also be used between close friends or lovers who want to reinforce their bond. Friends, for example, can greet each other with a ritual of handshake or other physical interaction or an inside joke. Lovers' connections are filled with these "insider" processes, each knowing how the other will respond and dancing through the ritual for mutual delight. Consider each of the steps of a ritual or process as if they were in a game as you craft new social processes and use them to spot existing ones.

Great game design considers the flow of emotions between participants, as described by game designer Nicole Lazzaro in 4 Keys to Fun. While it may not be a video game, crafting a social process also needs to consider how each person may feel during the process. How and when are celebrations shared? What social processes make people feel safe to make mistakes?

In the SAP developer network of several million members, there is a subset of about 150 highly engaged members called SAP Mentors, created by **Mark Finnern**. When they come to an event, there is a ceremony to welcome new mentors into the pack.

1. Members are asked to sing a song, lullaby or just "Happy Birthday."

2. Many want to resist, but as soon as they start or as soon as they finish, the rest of the mentors either pitch in or clap as appropriate.

A minute of discomfort sends a message that we can be foolish together and we will receive mutual support. That emotional journey of welcoming-in helps assure a sense of having passed from being outside to inside the group.

Jane McGonigal, author of _Reality Is Broken: Why Games Make Us Better and How They Can Change the World_, is a game designer focused on games that make a difference in our lives and in the world. She warns us though that games, and more importantly gamification, should not only be opt-in but also intrinsically motivated. Lots of organizations gamify behavior with extrinsic rewards: raises and bonuses, for example. Intrinsic rewards fuel a person's sense of self. For example, when you know you have mastered a task or activity, you feel intrinsically rewarded. When you get a badge or medal for it, you are being extrinsically rewarded.

Consider what makes your favorite ways to be playful so wonderful. Look at what social processes work. See if there are ways to bring game elements into social processes. The first attempts at this cross-pollination borrowed leaderboards and badges, which focus on extrinsic motivation and competition. See where you can take it with social processes that engage intrinsic motivation and cooperation.

There is an art to crafting social processes that engage participation. An example of artful parameters for interactions is Edgeryders' policy on community behavior.

Setting a High Bar

Nadia El-Imam helped found **Edgeryders**. It attracts people who already put themselves on the edge of mainstream society—who have the courage and desire to think and be different. Edgeryders is not fueled primarily by financial resources, but operates on a shared narrative, clear processes, and good tools. Social processes have been instituted to favor those who do the heavy lifting.

The online community has grown to 3,600 members in over 30 countries in 2016. They have principles for behavior rather than hard rules. Their "Edgiquette" reads:

> Edgeryders is a precious space for interaction to its community. We are proud to have somehow managed to build a space for learning safely about uncomfortable truths; for disagreeing respectfully; for asking for and freely giving help without this implying a pecking order. The rules governing interaction are those that you would expect when talking to people you deeply respect, and want to respect you too. Be clear and respectful. Don't be creepy.

Here (and elsewhere) they make it clear that this is a space for uncomfortable truths and respectful disagreement, which invites debate while asking for it to be well mannered. For the most part, they set the bar high not low. By which we mean, instead of low—saying all the things not to do—they set it high—be respectful and well mannered. These may seem vague. But when it then comes to enforcement, setting the bar high means that the questions to ask are not whether the behavior was *bad* but rather whether it was *good enough*. Asking people to be good enough invites them to step up, where asking them not to be bad simply ends in a debate about what constitutes bad behavior and allowing moderately bad behavior. This high bar is especially useful when encouraging people to be frank with each other in exposing the "elephant in the room."

Incentives

Within social process, we can add incentives to help "game" how the social process works. Incentives are indicators, metrics, and tokens that encourage actions and make flows visible. The best ones allow for self-steering.

The CEO and owner of the international temping and staffing agency, Randstad, noticed in the early days of the company that his sales offices were struggling to deal with the financial feedback they were getting. The company expanded quickly, more and more local offices were added, more agents were hired. The agents were selected for their interpersonal and commercial skills, being able to assess people applying for temp jobs and cater for customers. Their weakness was being able to read and understand P&Ls. And the P&Ls came 3 weeks or more after the end of the previous month. In a fast business like temping, 3 weeks is old news.

His solution (as an econometrist) was to design a simple and "good-enough" feedback indicator that anybody could apply immediately: the number of weekly hour-sheets from temps divided by the number of square meters in the local office. If that indicator was too low, you were in trouble and all the available commercial inventiveness was immediately put to work.

The rationale was clever. In temping, the average turnover per temp per week, and the gross margin on hours is surprisingly stable. Multiply this by the number of temp-weeks and you have your absolute gross margin. The vast majority of an agency's costs are staff wages. The number of staff is related to the size of the office. So you have an easy, quick, "80% or more correct" indicator that anybody could calculate and track, which scales from one office, to regions, to the whole company. No elaborate IT-system is needed.

The genius of his decision was that he created a compass that catered to the strengths and weaknesses of his staff. A compass that allowed them to steer themselves.

Tokens: making currents in the flow visible

Many processes do not need an object or a memory to function. But some are only made possible by adding a token or object to the interaction. In the US, we have social processes around giving tips to waiters, valets, and other service professionals. Money is the obvious example of an exchange that needs a token to function. A dollar bill represents an agreed value. That bill can be stored and transported to be used in another exchange, in another place and time, with another party that accepts the token as a representation of value.

Money is only one instance of this principle. There are many other implementations that have a different purpose. **Arthur Brock** designs alternative currencies or what he calls "Current-Sees." Current-Sees is a mnemonic to keep in mind that it is not (just) money but a method of making social flows and the processes associated with the flow visible, traceable, storable, and sometimes transferable.

Brock worked with Occupy Wall Street (OWS) to develop an ad-hoc, non-monetary Current-See:

We asked for a pressing problem they were currently experiencing. They told us about how the police were sending vagrants and people they released from jail down to OWS for free food, blankets, and camping supplies. Since OWS wanted to be open and inclusive, this meant a lot of people down there who were not necessarily respecting guidelines related to sobriety or quiet times for sleeping. Many of the activists now had difficulty sleeping through the night time noise and partying. But the topic was divisive and it was difficult to be clear if it was a widespread issue or only affecting particular places or people. Now this was a clear social flow problem we could work with!

We suggested that they introduce a simple coffee bean currency. Each morning in the breakfast line at the food table, as each person gets their food, ask them to indicate how well they slept by dropping a coffee bean in one of three jars with red/yellow/green lids. Each day there would be a clearly visible indicator of this particular aspect of wellbeing in the community for all to see. Now they can know when there's a major issue, or when there's scattered complaints. There's no need for complicated vote-counting, data collection, analysis or surveys, because feedback is incorporated into an existing process that adds 2 seconds, and you can eyeball the results. It yields an added bonus of everyone feeling like their voice and their wellbeing matters.

Brock differentiates between the aggregate behavior of individuals and the coherent behavior of social organisms (working within a membrane). The first is the sum of individual actions, while the latter creates the emergent behavior of the total social system. He specifically makes this distinction between two types of upper level flows in order to be clear about the different kinds of things that happen at the membrane layer. For example, traffic is an aggregate, whereas Occupy Wall Street is an aggregate with a membrane.

How is this "awareness" wired into organizations? Through the currencies we create as shared symbol systems to shape, enable, and measure value flows (think "Current-Sees" to keep in mind they're not just money). Current-Sees, like the one developed at OWS, are the nervous system of a social organism and one of the best ways to observe and to modify its pattern of awareness.

Use Case: Physical and Virtual

While a roundabout has a physical location and implementation, it does not mean that a physical design is a necessity for a social flow. For example, trading places in a queue needs a virtual tool, a Current-See.

Inland barges, which have to go through locks in rivers, have been treated on a first-come-first-served basis for ages. (The only exceptions are made for safety reasons—such as barges carrying dangerous goods—or when a big one that has priority cannot fit in, but a smaller one behind it does). But some barges have a need for speed, for instance trying to meet a deadline to get containers to a harbor to load on a seafaring vessel, while others earlier in line don't. Yet first-come, first-served will give priority to the barge with time to spare in this case.

A 'control and direct' approach would try to gather as much information as possible and design a priority allocation (algorithm or decision) tool. The authorities would decide who goes first.

A 'design the option space and the navigation' approach has resulted in a design that gives the captains of the barges a trading space and an alternative currency. The design is deceptively simple:

➢ A captain in a hurry can ask the ones before him in a queue to cede their priority.

➢ If the other captain agrees, he receives a credit from the one who gets priority.

➢ If necessary: repeat with the next one.

➢ At the lock, the authorities implement the agreed upon priority shift (no need to physically overtake any barge).

The simplicity of the rules reduces the threshold for everyone to participate. The introduction of a token (the credit) allows a trade anytime, anywhere, with anyone: if you receive a credit you can use it in an exchange with somebody else, in a different place and time. The rule that you have to ask for priority (meaning you cannot buy it) prevents negative behavior like hoarding credits and keeps the exchange in a social sphere where relationships matter: if you don't like the other guy who is asking, you can refuse. Another advantage of this setup is that you only need a sizable fraction to participate to be able to get the exchange rolling: no need for 100% participation. And the threshold to shift from bystander to participatant is very low. Participants make their own choices.

The governing body issues credits to get the exchange starting. Lock authorities can use the credits as well to influence behavior, as they discovered during the simulation.

This design for trading places in a queue has more potential: it is being investigated in other areas with queues and personal wishes, like in elderly homes: who is helped out of bed and washed first today?

In Part 4 we will further explore creating, measuring, and monitoring Current-Sees.

Crafting Social Processes

Triggers to add protocols

As with forms, social protocols are support tools that only need to be introduced where it's necessary to go beyond what is already naturally available to solve a problem. For instance, social protocols may be necessary when there are different, existing processes coming together that seem mutually exclusive. Or when irritation rises over time lost, misunderstanding one another, expectations that differ, or when caring levels drop or people have no time to build trust. It is always about interacting.

It can be as simple as this. When your daughter is leaving home to start her student life in college, you as parents have to find a balance between giving her room to grow on one hand, and checking if everything is going well on the other hand. What sometimes happens is that the parents progressively start to worry when time passes ("She still has not called...") and pour their anxiety into the phone when the daughter calls ("finally"). The daughter, who wasn't worrying at all about her parents, senses the anxiety, of course, and begins to dread the calls. Nobody is happy.

The social protocol solution is to agree upon a fixed moment in the week (say Sunday evening at 8pm) as the moment when to call and chat. Both sides can agree upon shifting the call to another moment, or skipping it because there are more pressing needs or little to talk about. No anxiety, clear expectations, and something everyone can look forward to.

Another social protocol could be putting your business card in the jar at a meeting every time you break the agreed meeting processes. Then at the end of the month, you buy lunch if you have the most cards in the jar.

Similarly, productivity is often interrupted by phone calls and meetings. While this might be fine for people in management or sales roles, others may need to immerse themselves deep in thought and can be quite frustrated by interruptions. It can take 20 minutes to return to work when you have to hold many ideas in mind at once (as with computer coders, for example). Is the social process currently in place one where creatives, developers, or other deep immersive workers can be interrupted? Is the expectation that they will stop, in the middle of a work session, to answer a phone or attend a meeting? A social protocol to solve this might be to have designated "immersive work" hours, where no meetings are scheduled. Or the phone is turned off with an auto reply that messages will be returned at break time. Or in open workspaces that someone with a headphone on should not be disturbed.

Also, look for <u>positive deviance</u>: where someone is doing something that works well that others are not doing. Maybe one coder on the team has a high output compared to others. What processes are they using to get time to focus? It might work for others, it might not, but usually a positive deviant is a good starting point.

Guidelines

We have found few guidelines for designing social process; it is a craft:

➢ What will help people set appropriate expectations. Is it a time or place that is standard?

➢ Look for where there is tension and create a process to reduce it.

➢ Find where people are not performing and why; see if a practice can assist in creating appropriate boundaries or procedures.

➢ Consider whether you are setting a high bar or a low bar.

Introducing New Process

There are a few approaches to introducing social protocols in a group:

> ➤ We can seed processes. Take meeting rituals. If people have a new experience of how to start a meeting and find it effective, they may use it in other meetings. If they see respectful dialogue on a website, they will often follow suit. We can encourage our online community to use 'yes, and' in debates, first through policy statements and then by community managers using 'yes, and' in their own comments.

> ➤ We can describe protocols in advance. That might be in our community policy, in our new employee or team member onboarding, or in the opening remarks for an event.

> ➤ We can train people to use processes, like giving people lessons in how to use Agile Methods.

> ➤ We can question habit: "Why are we always doing it this way? Is there no better/nicer/more agreeable way?"

Demonstration may not make the social process as clear, but it tends to have potent effect if done well. Dress codes are excellent, seemingly invisible social conventions: when here, wear this, in this way. Most of us can walk into a group and know what the appropriate clothing is. It might be described in the policy manual, but it is enforced by demonstration. We allow some outliers, but a sense of coherence on collective behavior is usually clear.

Summary for Social Processes

From our exploration of leading practitioners, we see the key guiding principles of process design are:

> ➤ Start by becoming sensitive to your own social processes that are so habitual that you have forgotten about them. Any new social process enters into a mature environment.

> ➤ Only add process when there is a need. And question existing protocols: are they just habit or do they have a clear purpose?

> ➤ Game design provides a good starting point for designing formal interactions: role, opt-in, goal, rules, progress indicators (where possible, intrinsic motivation).

> ➤ Tokens or alternative currencies make these protocols as flows visible, so everyone can contribute to coherent collective behavior.

> ➤ Processes need to be introduced carefully. Choose an introduction strategy and follow up.

Making Decisions

Probably the most complex question in a collective turns out to be: "how do we make decisions?" Perhaps because, in order to select an option, we have to have an agreement on how to select it. Perhaps, also, because with the ability to make decisions comes the power of movement and action using resources.

Even in networks of people without formal hierarchy, decisions have to be made, conflicts have to be resolved productively, tasks allocated. Many schools teach the traditional organizational structures (Mintzberg) as a solution; in practice people pick and choose from the archetypes.

Frederic Laloux points to the best practices of organizations where hierarchy has been limited as much as possible in order to reap the benefits of collective decision-making. His book is rich in practical advice and one of the best resources there is.

One key take-away from Laloux's book is that freedom comes with (uncomfortable) responsibilities. Responsibilities come with the need to hold one another accountable, which is an uncomfortable thing to do in a social group. A strict process creates the safe zone for confronting each other without damaging relationships.

H *During a management training we talked with a seasoned division manager of a large multinational. He told us about the integration of a product division they had acquired, in 20 countries. The portfolio, production, and sales locations and management teams of the acquired division and the existing business were overlapping, so they had to make decisions somehow on how to combine the two. He told us they had established two guidelines and committed themselves to them.*

One: for such a job you need your best people to investigate the issues and propose the decisions. The extra work puts pressure on them, which they can only bear for less than 9 months, preferably 6.

Two: to achieve the deadline of 6 months, top management (the division manager and his colleagues) had to force themselves to endorse decisions, and not fall into the trap of delaying and postponing. They themselves were considered the biggest risk in creating delays. So any proposal with options for decision that was submitted to them before 20.00, Friday, would get an answer by 08.00, Monday morning. The answer must be a choice for either one

> *of the options or another decision—anything but delays. Yes, they made mistakes, but in retrospect the cost of correcting mistakes was minute, far less than the cost of procrastination.*

The example shows an exceptional case: integration of two entities of this size is rife with conflict and dilemmas that can easily grow to a level where they overcome the capacity to deal with them, resulting in an internal attack, threatening the existence of the division. In this case, the priority has to be to prevent conflicts and dilemmas from getting out of hand. The entity has to get clarity and resolution as fast as possible: there's no time to lose. Hard decisions have to be made now, to prevent a crisis starting or escalating. An immune system has to kick in. Clear hierarchy and decisive leaders get you that. The risk is that decisive types will believe that there is always a crisis that requires decisive leaders who make detailed decisions. But decisive leaders of this kind are the last resort, they come at a high cost. The cost is that you sacrifice the benefits of a distributed, collective intelligence, which is far better and faster in innovating, adapting, dealing with unique circumstances, creating new solutions and complex behavior than a strict social hierarchy. Remember the "cost" of communicating in a hierarchy versus a network, which we talked about in the Introduction. The second cost is that some people will not find what they desire in their life and their work in a strict hierarchy: they suffocate in the hierarchical setup, get frustrated, and want to leave. Strong hierarchy is like chemotherapy: only to be used as a last resort against attack, when it is the lesser evil.

The challenge of evolving forms for people is to have both: even in networks of people without formal hierarchy, decisions have to be made, conflicts have to be resolved, tasks allocated. It is a conundrum for many. In practice people oscillate between archetypes:

> ➤ *Autocratic decision-making,* which fits well into hierarchy. It means top-down decisions by a leader.
>
>> • While this seems efficient, it may quickly ferment resistance from those implementing the decision, and it may not be the best-informed decision. It is good for panic situations, good for preventing cancerous growths, bad at collective development, and bad at dealing with a volatile, dynamic, and complex environment
>
> ➤ *Democratic decision-making,* where everyone votes and some percentage of agreement is reached.

- Elections are an example. This can be time-effective, however, it may not produce the best-informed decision and may lack actionable buy-in from voters. To increase engagement and commitment, there are variations on democratic decision-making that involve some degree of participatory process before voting.

➢ *Consensus decision-making*, where everyone agrees.

- It is flat, as everyone has the same amount of power in the decision. The process for consensus can be prohibitively long. However, once reached, commitment to the outcome tends to be high. There are methods of consensus that also involve participatory process to move the group more smoothly and quickly from divergence toward convergence.

➢ *Participatory decision-making*, where a process engages people in developing the decision together. This can unwrap the complexity of a decision and get a high degree of buy-in.

- This can be, in many but not all cases, time-consuming. The key difference between participatory and consensus decision-making is in how the process unfolds. This method starts at the roots, collectively navigating the problem space to build up to a collective decision, where consensus has focused on proposing a solution and working backwards to bargain the way toward a solution everyone can agree.

➢ *Polycentrism*, where a system has several centers, and leads to decisions that reflect the layer of the membrane at which they apply.

- This may use participatory, democratic, or consensus approaches. What matters is that the decision is made close to those affected by the decision, increasing the buy-in of those participating.

➢ *Chaotic*, where decisions are not clearly made in a known process or by a clear leader.

- This is the default method if no other process is clear. This can also mean that there is no accountability for decisions made, leading to poor ability to improve or learn from choices made. Buy-in tends to be low.

An example of highly effective decision-making can be found in Buurtzorg, the Dutch neighbor-care organization we discussed earlier. All new recruits and all new teams are required to take a course called "Solution-Driven Methods of Interaction." The course teaches them skills and techniques for collective decision-making, focusing on the basics of human collaboration: different styles of listening, different styles of communication, how to run meetings, how to coach one another, and many other practical skills.

Soft on Form, Hard on Process

For us, the most interesting practices relate to the way conflict is resolved and decisions made. How to steer between the two extremes of concentrated power within strong hierarchy on one hand, and perpetual indecision because anybody can object on the other. In all of Laloux's examples, the apparent "looseness" of the organizational form is balanced by the strictness of the decision-making. This is quite the opposite of the practice in strict hierarchies, where structure is hard and the process is hardly articulated. In successful self-steering organizations, form follows function, not the other way around.

The teams at Buurtzorg, for example, appoint a facilitator for meetings, who is there to observe and ask (the hard) questions. Group decisions can be made if no one has a principled objection; consensus is not required.

In all the organizations Laloux researched, from Buurtzorg, to die caster FAVI, to AES (a large, multinational energy company) there is an "advice-process." Anyone in the organization can make a decision, but it is mandatory that they first seek advice from ALL affected parties and from people with expertise on the matter. Advice must be sought and seriously considered. The bigger the decision, the wider the net must be cast. He lists these advantages of the advice process:

> ➢ It draws people whose advice is sought into the decision-making process, creating a community.

> ➢ Asking advice is an act of humility, making it very hard to ignore advice given.

> ➢ It is an on-the-job education for everyone involved.

> ➢ Chances are that a better decision will be made.

> ➢ It is fun for the advice seeker, spurring creativity and a sense of wellbeing.

The part to notice is that the final decision is not driven by the need for consensus. Consensus is seen as the road to tyranny of egos (everybody can hold a veto), and a dilution of responsibility for the decision taken. The organizations interviewed by Laloux feel that people make better decisions when they, and everybody else, knows they are responsible.

Dealing with Personal Conflicts in Decision-Making

What about conflicts? During the advice process someone may object vehemently to a proposed decision, there may be a dilemma over allocation of resources, colleagues may begin to irritate each other, or someone may be seen by peers not to be pulling their weight. For personal conflicts a strict conflict resolution process is essential.

> ➢ First a private conversation, with a clear proposal given by the initiator, which must be answered with yes, no, or a counterproposal.

> ➢ If that does not work, a colleague, whom they both trust, is asked to become a mediator.

> ➢ If mediation fails, a panel of topic-relevant colleagues is convened, to support resolution, but not to judge and decide.

> ➢ Ultimately the managing director joins the panel.

Only very rarely does this lead to a forced decision or dismissal, which is held to be a failure of the system. For professional conflicts or dilemmas (allocation of scarce resources) a similar but more collective process is used.

One key take-away from Laloux's book is that freedom comes with (uncomfortable) responsibilities. Responsibilities come with the need to hold one another accountable, which is an uncomfortable thing to do in a social group. A strict process creates the safe zone for confronting each other without damaging relationships.

Coherence for Flows

Governance

Governance (let's not call it management) becomes more and more necessary as an entity scales. Here we will explore how to govern its adaptation to scale and changing environments over time.

To continue to fit into the environment, we need processes and roles for auditing and maintaining the design itself. Remember how we talked about riding a bike not requiring an understanding of physics, just some simple feedback loops for course correction? Governance is one such feedback loop for course correction. Governance in an adaptive social organism is very different from the controlling and directing functions that make up governance in a static organization. The example of the roundabout versus the traffic light junction shows the difference between "controlling" (designing to *force a result*) versus "governing" (designing for a *flow to exist).*

We talk about culture as if it was a single thing, when actually it is different at different membrane layers. The culture of a team has unique qualities that may not be shared by a department or by the rest of the organization. Our team might be super strict about meeting start times or deadlines, but the organization may not be. There are micro-cultures, sub-cultures, and entity-wide cultures. Governance also fits to membrane layers.

Governance with a view to balancing the living social flow design is about:

> ➢ Developing rules and boundaries (what are the hard realities we want to operate within?)

> ➢ Developing guiding principles (what are the soft realities we want to be able to adapt around with each instance while honoring our purpose and values?)

> ➢ Monitoring the designed boundaries and rules to continue giving the desired improvement and shape of the flow.

> ➢ Adjusting the rules, principles, and boundaries when necessary.

> ➢ Or even stepping in to unblock a flow.

For instance: a roundabout may come to a complete stop if the amount of traffic is just too high: everybody is blocking everybody else. You need a traffic officer to step in and giving directions to get unstuck. The decision to send the officer is part of governance as well.

Quis custodiet ipsos custodes ~ who watches the watchmen?

The Roman poet Juvenal observed that governance is not one-dimensional but is layered: governance as a process needs governance of itself.

When we talk about governance as a part of culture and coherence, half the time we are talking about de-facto governance, expressed in social codes and social dynamics. We spoke with <u>Arno Hesse</u>, Founder of <u>Credibles</u>, who says "Official rules and control are often just an expression of the underlying values, beliefs, assumptions, and patterns. Corporate culture eats strategy for breakfast, because strategists often naively believe that they can re-chart the course and boundaries, just by proclaiming an intention or making a policy. That's when they get to experience the power of the culture's antibodies."

Nevertheless, explicit expression in rules and agreements is useful when scaling up or out, for keeping flows operational in lower-trust environments and so on. When operationalizing we also are talking about this explicit governance: the explicit rules and agreements, and how to change them.

Cultivating Good Governance

Governance is about the implicit and explicit rules or principles we apply to ourselves and our joint activities, both to our process and to our new or modified flows. The early seeds of governance emerge from the narrative and the structure of relationships between the people doing reframing together. In the narrative, what relationship to authority, agency, or autonomy does each role have, and how do the different roles relate to one another?

Values show up here. This is where early agreements are formed between those who want to reframe or the one who does and his or her first allies; these may be different from the agreements of an organization or coalition that forms later. This stage of governance development reflects more of how the seed can be grown into an ecosystem. And deciding that there are no rules to start with is also one governance option.

We noted from our research that a small, tight-knit group may be heavy on consensus or heavy on hierarchy, rooted in a shared vision at the beginning in order to ensure coherence of the idea. Then, as the idea expands, the structure may evolve into one with a different approach to cooperation. The first steps often require some implicit or explicit form of leaderfulness—the initiative to take a step, suggest an idea, or push an agenda, which later may flip to invitation and openness as the reframing garners larger attention and participation. However, in almost all cases, we see emerging clarity about how the small circle of people clustered around an idea can interact with one another.

One potential pitfall to avoid is over-designing governance, worrying too much in the beginning about governance that will be needed over the lifespan of the development. Rules can quickly become anchors for the unsure, and barriers for the bold.

It is not necessary, nor even desirable, to make the governance of the seed consistent with the governance of the eventual affiliation of the community for that seed. It can help to think of it as a transition opportunity. The early core needs to protect and nurture the seed in a world that is resistant to it. This is different from the process of growing and expanding that seed. One can also think of it as the difference between how the board or advisory council governs itself and how the larger organization or community that it serves is governed.

The clearer we can make the transition from the protective environment of a greenhouse for sprouting the seed and the outdoor conditions of the garden, with its requirements of surviving and thriving in, the better.

Let's look at the example of **Edgeryders**. The organization first formed with a small group of people with funding from the Council of Europe and European Commission. Within two years it moved away from that container to become a purely volunteer-driven community. The early team set firm parameters for what they wanted Edgeryders to be and how it would work and what relationship it would have to the funding organization. Over time, as the online community and event platform the team built focused on participatory engagement, the community began to take over and collectively direct the course of events. From the community the idea of Unmonasteries was sparked, where communities and makers could develop mutually beneficial arrangements. Now annual events (LOTE—Living on the Edge) and the online community self-direct the course of action while being guided and supported by the initial committee that formed the organization.

Governance during the reframe is about setting and creating the initial conditions for the idea to grow and take shape. What matters is that the values implicit in the narrative are being honored in designing what is to come.

Designing Explicit Governance

In *Governing the Commons*, Nobel-prize winner Elinor Ostrom tells about ancient and recent cooperatives that have developed rules for stable, century-long cooperation to use and protect commons like water sources, mountain grasslands, or fishing grounds—at the same time refuting the idea of the "tragedy of the commons." These cooperatives fill the gap between "government" and "private company" and achieve results that both of these struggle to achieve themselves. Ostrom noted eight principles that enable this success:

➢ Define clear group boundaries.

➢ Match rules governing use of common goods to local needs and conditions.

➢ Ensure that those affected by the rules can participate in modifying the rules.

➢ Make sure the rulemaking rights of community members are respected by outside authorities.

➢ Develop a system, administered by community members, for monitoring members' behavior.

➢ Use graduated sanctions for rule violators.

➢ Provide accessible, low-cost means for dispute resolution.

➢ Build responsibility for governing the common resource in nested tiers from the lowest level up to the entire interconnected system.

The ground rules she discovered show boundaries (mechanisms to be in or out), immune systems (how to discipline someone or force out a bad apple) and governance agreements on how to adapt. And, last but not least, the need for recursiveness, how to embed a local chapter into a bigger ensemble, how to get protection from the bigger ensemble to be able to survive as an entity.

This is flow expressed in guidelines. These guidelines are a good starting point for any entity that thinks about its own form, flow, and governance.

Rule-based or principle-based

The expansion of the Roman Empire created a governance challenge: how to create and maintain a more or less unified societal structure over vast distances, when it took months to travel to the outskirts of the Empire. The answer was to create Roman law: a system that established general principles instead of precise rules. The task of local government was to implement the principle, to allow local interpretations and variations as long it was in the spirit of the law. Magistrates and judges placed higher value on the fact that someone had followed the spirit of the law, than on strict obedience to rules—if the latter would lead to results that went against the general principle.

This idea is still dominant in many (European) countries that once were under Roman rule. For instance, contracts in those countries may hold the clause that someone is expected to act in good faith or be a good steward.

Breaking that clause can be brought to court, where a judge will decide whether this has been the case or not. Clauses in contracts that go against general principles can be nullified afterwards.

The tribes that were not conquered by the Romans (notably the Saxons) continued with their so-called natural law system, based on rules. You are not allowed to break the rules, anything else is allowed. This has been continued in the Anglo-Saxon world and implemented in the law system of countries with Anglo-Saxon roots. According to Jaap Peters, it leads, for example, to much larger and more detailed contracts than in the Roman law system, as all circumstances that can be imagined must be described in rules.

It may be a good exercise for everyone involved to consider what unconscious assumptions they hold that reflect a background in either rule-based or principle-based environments. A potential bias may influence the design of the governance adversely.

In the realm of control, we create hard and fast rules, which then get continuously clarified in an additive process. In the realm of swarms and adaptive behavior, it pays to create principles and boundaries trusting each participant to navigate the space using those principles the vast majority of the time.

Holacracy for Social Flow Governance

One interesting variation not mentioned by Laloux is Holacracy (and Sociocracy on which it is based). **Brian Robertson**, founder of HolacracyOne, offers Holacracy as an organizational structure that emerges from purpose to evolve governance over time.

Holacracy starts with a governance process to achieve purpose and then lets the form evolve. The shape emerges from the combination of Roles, with their associated Purposes, acting over Domains and with Accountabilities that evolve as they go.

Evolution in the organization is triggered by tensions voiced by people in their Roles. A tension is seen by Prashant Mittal as a tell-tale sign of potential growth and evolution, as a by-product of the organism evolving and growing in its environment:

A moral, reasonable or rational purpose of governance aims to assure (on behalf of others) that an organization produces a worthwhile pattern of good results while avoiding an undesirable pattern of bad circumstances. It conveys the process-oriented elements of governing.

While a Domain grants your Role a property (authority and accountability), it does not grant you a property right (ownership). Your responsibility, should you choose to accept a Role in a Holacracy-powered organization, is one of *steward*—you are controlling the Role not for your own sake, but for its sake. Think of it like having power of attorney. You are acting on behalf of the person or thing rather than *being* the person or thing. Your job is to control the property that belongs to the Role, and use the authority of the Role for the sake of its Purpose, which then serves its Circle's Purpose, which ultimately then serves the whole organization's Purpose. This one layer of abstraction creates a slight distance between people and roles that reduces the play of egos and engages care and concern.

Holacracy is a membrane-oriented form with a focus on process and governance. The interpersonal politics of participating in Holacratic organizations are quite different from more traditional structures, so people joining these new organizations must be able to adapt to the new approach.

Governing Principles

From our discussions with, and analysis of, leading practitioners, we see the key guiding principles of governance design are:

> ➢ Even very simple processes for interaction can lead to rich and complex interactions, once you make room for individual agency and a large number of (social) relationships between people.

> ➢ Fewer rules means more freedom for agency. Use principles instead, and provide context and feedback: roundabouts do not function in midair for jet planes.

> ➢ Quick and easy to grasp feedback is essential for learning and adapting, to find your own path as a participant in all the options and all situations. Easy navigation (when necessary, aided by sophisticated IT) offsets choice anxiety.

> ➢ Rely on our innate ability to experiment and learn: by doing, receiving feedback, and adapting our heuristics we are able to deal with mathematically complex realities: we don't need to understand the physics to be able to catch a baseball while running.

> ➢ Not all conflicts can be resolved by rules; not everybody abides by the rules. Governance needs to create a mechanism to enforce playing by the rules and principles, and solving conflicts/stalemates

that get out of hand. Your immune system will do the actual work, while governance creates the process for it.

> Simulate and test: people will continue to surprise you with their ingenuity and resourcefulness. This includes learning to extract maximum benefit from a system but also means that all systems will be gamed—sometimes in ways that are detrimental to the whole. Select the threshold of tolerance for that.

> Principles, rules and designs need to evolve over time as society evolves. Keep in touch with reality, design your own tell-tales and feedback that will warn when the rules become out-of-date.

> Governance is a leadership role, best separated from individual (partial) interests, but supported by all players.

Use Case: the AMS-IX

The governance of the Amsterdam Internet Exchange (AMS-IX) has been one of the key factors in its growth and success, as measured by the high value that its more than 650 participants place in it. An Internet Exchange is a physical place where independent networks (ISPs, etc.) gather to interconnect with each other and exchange packets for their subscribers. Using an Exchange is not mandatory, nor can it be enforced. Usually big ISPs create a direct link between their networks at their convenience: the IX is used to facilitate easy and cheap interconnection with many smaller networks.

It is much easier to manage one interface with an IX with published rules of engagement, than to manage a multitude of interfaces, each with a different party. Mathematically it is easy to see that the number of direct interfaces explodes, if the number of parties that want to interconnect with each other grows. If 10 parties want to interconnect directly with each other, that's already 45 links!

An IX works best (from the perspective of the networks who are its customers) if:

> many interesting networks (with interesting websites your customers want to reach) and many services like Google and YouTube and Facebook have a presence at the IX

> the IX innovates to keep up with fast moving demands

➢ the interconnect is reliable, flexible, high performance and cheap

➢ the IX acts neutral, does not give unfair advantages to anyone, does not mess with the traffic

Let's analyze the governance structure of the AMS-IX on our guiding principles:

➢ Governance is a leadership role, best separated from individual (partial) interests, but supported by all players.

The governing body of the AMS-IX is an Association. Any customer who wants to use the services automatically becomes a member of the Association. The Association is the sole owner of the limited company that operates the platform. The management of the limited company leads in proposing investments, decision, prices, and so on, but the Association decides as a whole.

All Association members are transparent about costs and pricing, have decision power on proposed investments, services, and price-structures, but have to come to a consensus first to be able to make decisions.

➢ Governance must create a mechanism to enforce the rules and principles, and solve conflicts/stalemates that get out of hand.

The Association is a formal legal structure with articles that describe its goal and governance rules. One key part of an Association under Dutch law is that members—not just the board—are legally responsible for the collective.

➢ Quick and easy to grasp feedback is key to learning and adapting. Members are free to use the platform's services, or not. This encourages management to listen closely to what members need and adapt to make it easier and cheaper for members to use the IX than go their own way. Fewer rules mean more freedom for agency.

➢ Simulate and test. The IX has limited itself to providing cheap, reliable, and easy connectivity for its members, which has attracted a lot of players. The fast development of services on the Internet and the changing roles of players has created new demands, which are tested and deployed on demand.

Flows and Coherence: Conclusion

Growing a form means applying these practices in a custom manner, fit for the task: cultivating. The most important step is to be conscious of these three factors—social processes (including incentives), decision-making, and governance—when cultivating the flow, and look for examples and experiences to build upon.

When thinking about social protocols, it can help to learn from game design. For example, does it clearly have a role for each person to play, is it optional, does it have a goal, are the rules clear, and do we know if we are making progress or it is working? Sometimes it also helps to add incentives, whether that is a token to be played or a metric to show progress.

In crafting social protocols, we can look for triggers to see if they might be needed. We offered a few guidelines and some ways to introduce protocols.

There are many different kinds of processes to use in making decisions. What we found social flows use is form and clear process rather than relying on roles (where we can fall into chaotic decision-making processes). We offered some tips on dealing with conflicts that arise from decision-making.

Governance has an important role, to be separated from the process and particular subsets of stakeholders. It helps if all stakeholders feel represented by the governance body. Governance can be rule-based or principle-based, it also helps to be aware of the difference and be explicit about the intent. We suggest being mindful of who watches the watchers and thus have process for evolving governance over time.

Governance can even be used to allow an organizational structure to emerge from purpose and to evolve over time. Evolution is triggered by tensions: a tension should be seen as a tell-tale sign of potential growth and evolution, as a by-product of the organism evolving and growing in its environment.

On CultivatingFlows.com we list examples we receive from practitioners, and links to relevant literature. What have you discovered in your practice around protocols, process, and governance? Share with others on the website.

Quick Guide to Flows and Coherence

Social Protocols

Protocols create safety and predictability in interactions, even between strangers. Become sensitive to your own social protocols.

Is there a process guide, norming behavior or legislation of behavior? Most social protocols are habits we don't even think about (which, by being invisible, can make them a source of unwitting conflict when cultures clash). Humor can help as an indicator and a lubricator.

Crafting social protocols that engage participation is an art. We can learn from the process of designing games. How does the social process create a role, provide options to play, set a goal to achieve, give ground rules for behavior, and update participants with progress indicators?

> ➢ Agile Methodologies with the Standup meeting is an example.

> ➢ Other examples include rituals and rites of passage.

Incentives

Incentives are indicators, metrics, and tokens that encourage actions and make flows visible. The best ones allow for self-steering.

Tokens are a specific subset that make flows visible, countable, and possible to be taken to another moment and place. They can be nicknamed "Current-Sees," a powerful tool to enhance flows.

Guidelines for designing social process:

> ➢ Use the 4 Keys to Fun to engage emotions.

> ➢ Use intrinsic motivation where possible.

> ➢ Set appropriate expectations. Is it a time or place that is standard?

> ➢ Notice triggers: look for where there is tension and create a process that reduces the friction, or look for underperformance and create process or incentives to address it.

> ➢ Find where people are not performing and why, then see if a practice can assist in creating appropriate boundaries or procedures.

➢ Consider whether you are setting a high bar or a low bar. Set a high bar, so behavior is judged against what is most desirable rather than compared to the worst.

Introducing New Process

➢ Seed processes, like meeting rituals, for example. If people have a new experience of how to start a meeting, and they find it effective, they may carry it into other meetings.

➢ Describe protocols in advance.

➢ Train people to use processes, like giving people lessons in how to use Agile Methods.

➢ Question habits: "Why are we always doing it this way? Is there no better/nicer/more agreeable way?"

Making Decisions

➢ Freedom and responsibility are intricately linked.

➢ Different decision-making strategies are useful in different circumstances. Carefully choose when to use which.

➢ Autocratic, democratic, consensus, participatory, polycentric, or chaotic

Be soft on form, hard on process: consider using an advice process, distinguishing who makes decisions and is held accountable from who is consulted on decisions and influences the choice (and supports the results).

➢ Deal with personal conflicts in decision-making:

• Have a process to de-escalate with collaborators and a stairstep process to ratchet up to higher forms of intervention.

• A strict process actually helps us hold each other accountable safely.

Governance for Coherence

Governance: how you are collectively able to adapt, test, and modify behaviors, accountability, and how to deal with exceptions and disasters.

➢ Governance with a view to balancing the living social flow design is all about:

- rules and boundaries
- guiding principles
- monitoring and learning
- adjusting
- unblocking flow

➢ Culture fits to membrane layers: micro-culture, sub-culture, organization culture, etc.

➢ Who watches the watchmen? Legislating behavior is dangerous to impose, but the shared clarity of expectations is helpful.

➢ Designing explicit Governance

- use Ostrom's 8 Principles for Managing a Commons
- notice whether governance is rule-based or principle-based

CHAPTER 7:

SUPPORTING TECHNOLOGY

"One man's magic is another man's engineering."

Social flows and social technology, for us, are all about supporting humans as we are. And we are not machines running programs. However, physical and information technology can support social flows and help ideas scale. You might call it: augmenting swarm behavior.

Amplifying and Enabling Social Flows

About a century ago, a band of young physicists ripped the curtains away from Newtonian physics. The new models, as formulated by Einstein and his contemporaries, proved to be vastly superior: not only did they confirm the Newtonian models and explain the "minor" aberrations in observations, they modeled nature successfully beyond what our human senses can observe: at one extreme at the size of our universe and at the other extreme at the size of the atom or smaller. Experimentation confirmed the models and a slew of new technologies was and is being developed as a result.

It is hard to overestimate the effect these new technologies have had and still have on society. The list is long: all the ubiquitous and portable computing power supplied by semiconductors and integrated circuits, lasers and LEDs and flat screens, fiber optics for worldwide telecommunication (Internet), sophisticated sensors for measuring and analysis which have benefited medical science and life sciences and the development of new materials, nuclear technology (including many applications beyond power generation and armaments) and so on.

Advances in telecommunication which have culminated in the Internet, and advances in traveling (most of all cars and jet planes) have had a secondary effect: they have enabled social flows to go beyond previous constraints: of time and place, of physical contact limited by costly and slow means of travel, of slow communication by letter and telegram, of one-to-many mass media like newspapers, books, radio, and TV.

It is hard to imagine how limited the possibilities of social flow were in daily life for previous generations, compared to what we find normal now.

The unprecedented adoption rate of the technology that opened the door to these social interactions shows what a huge void was filled. Clearly innovations in physical and information technology have influenced social flows. But are we intentionally innovating to augment human abilities and assist in social flows?

Social Technology uses Physical Technology

Social technology often uses physical technology as much as anything. Physical technologies are supposed to augment our strengths and support us in overcoming our weaknesses. Tools that visualize complex datasets with interrelated dependencies help us to apply our amazing capacity to see patterns in otherwise mind-numbing rows of numbers and formulas. Databases and calendars support our limited capacity for memorizing data. You could even argue that we have a talent for adapting physical technology and repurposing it to fill a need in social technology. Texting by phone was never intended to be used as it was. And the hashtag on Twitter was invented by a user.

Twitter started in 2006. It was a mix of text messages and short posts then. It was easy to post and easy to follow the people you knew and wanted to listen to. But it was hard to have a discussion or talk with like-minded people. You couldn't do a "group" or have a "community" there in 2007.

In August of 2007 this epic post appeared. It changed Twitter forever into a fluid, self-organized set of conversations and groups.

> **how do you feel about using # (pound) for groups. As in #barcamp [msg]?**
>
> 12.25 PM August23, 2007 from PocketTweets

 Mr Messina

<u>Chris Messina</u> proposed the hashtag to denote groups. He posted to his blog about it, and it took off like wildfire. We now take it for granted; it has become part of our culture. You see hashtags on billboards and packaging.

The proposal of the hashtag was deceptively simple yet purposefully designed. Historically, information has been organized by hierarchical taxonomy. Tagging was becoming popular as a Web 2.0 form of Folksonomy—an emergent form of taxonomy that includes synonyms. Hashes had been a practice in IRC (Internet Relay Chat) to define channels.

Combining the channel idea of using a hash or pound sign with the popular concept of tagging, Chris Messina suggested the hashtag. He had clearly thought through a ton of social protocol, and listened to a lot of the wisdom of other practitioners in the field to discern what criteria ought to be met and how to test if this could solve the challenges at hand. If you read his descriptions, it is clear he thought about the flow and operationalized it with one simple social hack. He even thought about self-healing and protection against attacks. He thought about what sort of governance method the social protocol enabled. In his description on Quora he writes, "If spammers ended up taking over a hashtag due to popularity, the ease with which hashtags are created enabled non-spammers to abandon the hashtag and move on quickly. Indeed, the very ephemerality of hashtags is what makes them easy and compelling to use in a fast-moving communication medium like Twitter."

When Chris Messina proposed the hashtag on twitter, he had no idea how fast it would propagate across the Internet. What was then a social hack—adding the pound sign to indicate a tag, channel, or group—has since become a hard-coded technology that machines can process on our behalf. See Storify.com as an example: it gathers all the posts with a hashtag, and lets you edit the story to produce a meaningful stream. Machines and a good social protocol work together to help us to navigate the enormous and rich flow of conversations that our social brains could not otherwise handle.

Mechanical technology, information technology, and even AI technology enable social protocols at a much greater distance in space or time. They let a social protocol go to vast scale. They enable collaboration where it could not happen before, particularly with large networks of people.

Physical or information technology can support or stifle the development of social technology. In our experience, the key difference is to start thinking in process hierarchies as opposed to functional hierarchies.

Designing physical or information technology for process hierarchies requires a different mindset than designing a new machine for a machine bureaucracy. When IT systems are designed to enforce the way in which information flows, designed to force people into a fixed process where they perform a standardized part, they empower the functional hierarchy and increase the level of hierarchical functional control. The technology augments the functional hierarchy, with mind-numbing results for its victims.

The same IT could be used to empower the same people to act. The example of ENE in Chapter 4 (Care Brabant) shows how technology puts tools in people's hands to navigate complexity, the complexity of choosing individual care protocols. The hierarchy is still there, but it is of a different kind: maintaining the tools is one level, choosing the free space and the limitations the tools will give access to is another level.

Designing Machines for Humans

Good old voice telephony. We probably never realized that we took the flaws and limitations of the technology for granted because it gave so much back in benefits. Only thinkers like <u>Martin Geddes</u>, a telecom consultant, kept pointing out that the standard service was sorely lacking in supporting social flows, in social cues that are normal between people. He gives this example:

> *You know that your wife has had a rough time with the kids being ill, she has had little sleep at night. Is she taking a sorely needed nap in the afternoon? You don't want to wake her for something that is not very urgent, that can wait an hour or so. What if you could send a text-message that is silent, does not trigger a notification because you command it not to do so? What if you could call directly to voicemail, bypassing the ringing of the phone? What if you could send a voicemail or text with delayed notification ('Notify the one called if not read within 2 hours after sending')? All options could have been supported using old-school phones, landline, and mobile.*
>
> *More sophisticated options that require smartphones are status indicators. Like indicating to potential callers, or specific groups of callers if you are either a) open for calls, b) open for calls after 11.00 (when the meeting you are in is finished) or leave a voicemail, c) only to be called in emergencies, unless you are family or boss.*

While these features would have been useful to us, hardly anyone implemented them. The incumbent operators were gatekeepers of technology change. No wonder applications like WhatsApp, which allow you a much richer set of social cues and protocols, have become so popular so quickly. Designing for social flows beats things that are not augmenting our ability to have relationships and get things done cooperatively.

We want to know what someone is doing before we interrupt them, but we don't typically get access to that information to then make appropriate choices about interrupting, coming back, or leaving a message. For some people, calling even has become socially unacceptable unless invited, prearranged, or as an emergency: you first agree via other media to call each other before pressing the button. A ringing phone is an intrusion, harassment unless you have been invited to enter that private space.

So much technology is designed to be convenient for business and profitability and merely sufficient to attract "users" to it rather than really creating ways to enhance our lives (without having to switch programs, tools, and enter our password again). However, technology that helps social flows wins again and again, as the Social Era is demonstrating. Imagine, for example, if you had one login (it might have deeper security measures for your bank than for your newspaper subscription), but you didn't have to know dozens of passwords and could move fluidly from one online portal to another. Imagine if you took your social network with you instead of having to re-create it on every new social application.

Innovations like these are being worked on. The way we store information might be changing to allow more fluidity. Reputation across various sharing economy applications like Airbnb, Lyft, and Uber could also arrive. To the degree that developers don't create it for us, are there ways that we, as "users" can hack it like Chris Messina did, to serve our social flow? What might we consider when designing for social flow, using supporting technologies?

➤ Does the technology enrich context and meaning?

➤ Focus on "support" in supporting technologies, helping humans do what we are best at and transcend our limitations. How do our social flows need augmentation to scale or serve us better?

➤ Playing with the mixing board of options to tune into what works for our desired social flow.

We will address each of these now.

Add Context and Meaning

Technology retains data but not context—and context is value. In most conversations the words "data" and "information" are used as loose, generic terms, as if they are interchangeable. And Big Data is a magical term promising unknown treasures hidden in vast data sets.

But when you look at data as a communication tool, supporting social flows between entities, a more rigorous and richer definition of data appears. Communicated data can be seen as having three nested properties:

> ➤ the message itself

> ➤ the meaning of the message

> ➤ the value of the meaning

Conveying a message relies on an agreed protocol for syntax and semantics so you can decode the data into a message.

Imagine that data transmitted reads as "Ack. Nuts. 1000"

> ➤ Does "Ack" mean:
>   - Acknowledgment of reception of message and this is a repeat?
>   - This is responding to a request how many are in stock?

> ➤ Does "nuts" mean:
>   - something you can eat?
>   - a thing you combine with a bolt to fasten two items together?
>   - someone who has mental problems?

> ➤ Is the unit of "1,000":
>   - dollars?
>   - gallons?
>   - seats?

Agreements on syntax and semantics allow you to understand that the intent meaning is (for example): "Yes, we have 1000 M6 nuts in stock"

The meaning of the message is context-dependent. Usually sender and receiver share some context. When your partner sends you a message "pick up a loaf of bread will you?" there is an implicit understanding which type of bread she/he would like (whole grain), and where to buy it (the small bakery you both love). The shared context developed by sharing lives gives a specific meaning to the message.

Even the absence of data in a message can be of great meaning, given a certain context. If Customs and Immigration miss certain fields in a declaration of import, alarms may go off if the context warrants increased alertness (for instance the origination of a container and its declared destination, combined with what is supposed to be in there, and the timing). Many inventions are triggered by the absence of expected data. The core traffic management method of the Internet is based on the absence of data.

The key insight here is that the same message can have multiple meanings, dependent on the context shared by sender and multiple receivers. Each receiver may have his/her own context. The same form that triggered Customs, is of little interest to the Harbor authorities responsible for traffic management or the container terminal planning storage capacity.

The third level is the value of the meaning of the message. Again, value is highly particular to either the sender or the receiver(s). "Agreed" may mean for the sender (a big company) just another purchase order, and for the receiver (a start-up) a breakthrough. A reading of a water level along a river may have little value for the farmer who records it, but may have meaning for the city downstream that an impending flood can be averted.

The Internet of Things threatens to swamp us with vast quantities of data. We need software to manage notifications and be smart enough to know the value of the data provided. I want to know if my home is burning down right away, but I don't want to be alarmed by my housemate burning toast. I want my personal assistant to warn me before I leave the house that I should leave early to avoid the construction or accident on my commute, to anticipate my flow and possibly notify my first meeting I am running late. These social flows can be designed so that each person is supported in their flow as well as all of us together having a sense of how to swarm around the traffic jams.

Tools like <u>microformats</u> (a way of structuring data that retains metadata) can help data move through different spaces and retain sufficient context, and then have appropriate interfaces that give value to that contextualized data in ways that help us (each of us might value different aspects more highly).

Focus on Support

Supporting Technologies for social flow provide support to humans as we are (distracted, forgetful, creative, quick to learn, differently motivated, etc.). Humans are good at working with others who are very much like us, but not as good at working with people with different values or other differences. Software can help us cooperate with each other across this gap, which in person might produce friction.

Valdis Krebs, Chief Scientist at Orgnet.com, claims that total sameness (maximal alignment) means that adding people does not add value, but total difference means we can't even communicate with each other. We need diversity of skills, vision, goals, etc., to generate value together; but we also need to be able to communicate and organize together. He uses a maxim to capture this: connect on your similarities and profit from your differences.

Use Case: Collaboration before Alignment

Enter **Mushin Schilling** and **Anne Caspari,** who contributed an essay to our research. They overturn the popular notion that we should first have unity before we can take action. They claim that collaboration does not require unity, or even community; rather it needs transparency and flow leadership. The smallest unit of work is a task. Collaborative support systems give transparency about who takes what task, about what now needs to be done, and record in augmented memory what has been learned. When the group or project does its business, guided by flow leadership, consensus is not needed. Nobody needs to be asked for permission before collaborators move ahead. It is enough that a move is transparent, so that all collaborators know what is going on and who is doing what, and can themselves choose where they want to contribute and when. Smoothing the potential social friction, the software enables this unaligned collaboration. Schilling and Caspari design software (worknets) that enables such collaboration without alignment. Through this software, we can reach scales of collaboration—without alignment—that we could not have reached before. Designing such software requires careful configuration of a range of options.

When people do not share values or culture, there can be friction and misunderstandings. To reduce this, we often try to homogenize organizations. However, that creates a monoculture which is less creative and resilient. So, Schilling and Caspari offer software to mediate between contributors, reducing friction while increasing resilience.

Mixing Board for Supporting Technologies

Kevin Marks has been inventing and innovating for over 25 years in emerging technologies where people, media, and computers meet. He lays out some of the questions and considerations for designing social software knobs and dials, showing how different settings are appropriate for different tools. He discusses the delay in response (latency) that different communication media tolerate: we expect a response to a voicemail within a day, but that would be out of tolerance for a WhatsApp message. Then he explores persistence. And thus we begin to build the mixing board for supporting technologies. We might have instant but not persistent, such as WhatsApp, or we might have latent and persistent like handwritten and mailed letters. Both can serve a human need and a social flow. Which serve the flows we are working on?

Should these communications be public or private? We are adjusting to a lot of information that used to be private being publicly visible, while other information is constrained to certain publics (e.g. only friends of friends on Facebook). When I use Google search, I get a different result than you do because it is customized to me. Similarly on social media, the content is always already filtered. No two people are seeing the same public content.

These publics overlap to varying degrees without discrete sets. We all have different experiences of them and their intersections. Because this is all more flowing and more abundant, there is a shift in behavior. We used to want to answer every call. Then we wanted an answering machine to pick up the calls we missed. Then we wanted the answering machine to pick up for us so we could screen calls. Similarly, online, the flow of a tools like Twitter is so vast that we don't want to absorb the whole of our stream; instead we dip into the flow and out again. Our expectations change.

Marks explores several other dimensions of online communication flows such as whether we see a picture of the person with the communication or not and whether our connections are two-way and person-to-person or not (Facebook used to be, Twitter never was). It can help to draw a map of a slice of the flows that will support the scaling of a social design and consider what adjusts the speed, width, and dimensionality of the communication.

Marks doesn't dictate which are best; instead he highlights the consequences of one choice over another for different goals. Using digital and physical technologies to extend social technology is best done by considering the parameters of the design of the social element. Also, the rapid prototyping call to "sense, design, test, and scale" applies here.

Unintended Consequences

Our efforts to scale often have unintended consequences. With Supporting Technology this is visible in the way the Internet has become a playground for trolls and malicious comments. Still, we can continue to innovate to enhance social flows. For example, CivilComments.com is hoping to provide a solution to that unintended consequence of increased interactivity. CivilComments uses a social flow design as a response, similar to our roundabout. People have to look each other in the eye, and let those who are already in flow go through. In CivilComments' case, that means readers can give preference to people who have other highly-rated, peer-reviewed comments. It may still be working on the precise settings for the tool, but having other commenters rating comments in order to try to post their comment might work. It is certainly infinitely scaleable, adaptable to a community's culture, and doesn't require costly staff oversight and moderation.

Supporting Technology: Conclusion

Taking Social Flows to a New Level

Technology allows us to take social flows to a new level and scale. However, most information technology sends data rather than sharing context and meaning. We can work around this data limitation to share metadata and design interfaces that provide meaning to enhance our social flow.

Supporting Technologies can be designed to work with humans as we are, given our strengths and weaknesses, augmenting our abilities. For example, Worknets allow us to collaborate before we have unity of values.

The thing to remember when using physical and information technology is that it is still supporting a social flow, so the designer should be very aware of the social knobs and dials present and select carefully and test often. Twitter is a good use case on how seemingly simple design features make a huge difference to social flows in practice. Those who enable better social flows will persist (and AI is the next way we will be doing this at broad scale).

And it is critically important to remember that we are still dealing with flows, not static systems. They are evolving. For example, Twitter created the "follower count" metric and software developers leveraged this to create information about reach and influence of a given tweeter. But those systems have to keep evolving as people "game" the metric and thus the results of the algorithm are less and less useful unless they evolve ahead of the tools for gaming them.

At CultivatingFlows.com, add your wisdom on supporting technology for social flow, or see what others have to say. Our understanding grows when we all share what we are learning and how we are evolving.

Quick Guide to Supporting Technology

Amplifying and enabling social flows

The most expansive and disruptive potential is created by allowing people to create protocols, meaning, and value, without asking anybody for permission.

> ➢ Example: Hashtags created by a user on Twitter to enable social flow. Then the social protocol of tagging feeds back into information technology so that Storify.com can organize content for us to tell stories over numerous posts and multiple contributors.

> ➢ Use physical and information technology to augment our human strengths and weakness to enable social flows.

> ➢ Physical and information technology has influenced social flows tremendously. And we have hacked them to help us too. Physical and information technology can be used to help people navigate complexity.

Designing machines for humans

Companies often design for profit rather than for human experience. This is changing, because what is designed for social flows wins.

> ➢ A much richer set of social cues and protocols drives the popularity of applications.

> ➢ Still, so much is designed to be easy for business and not for social flows. But what *does* support the #SocialEra will win.

Add Context and Meaning

> ➢ Technology stores data, not context or meaning.

> ➢ Value resides in shared context and varies by participant or group.

> ➢ To help people navigate, provide context that matters to them in a way that honors what they find valuable.

> ➢ Social flows supported by (information) technology require you to think explicitly about the levels of data/protocol —> meaning and value.

> ➤ Filter data and present what is meaningful and valuable.

Focus on support—augment humans as we are

> ➤ Make sure there is enough difference to benefit from connection, enough commonality to be able to communicate: connect on similarities and profit from differences.

> ➤ Worknets help unaligned groups be productive on shared goals through transparency about what is done and what remains to be done, where software is the buffer zone.

Play with the Mixing Board

> ➤ Think about the various knobs and dials of physical and information technologies and how each can be set to optimize social flows:

> - latency
> - public or private
> - identity expression
> - connection types
> - persistent or not...

> ...to adjust the speed of the flow and behavior within it.

Unintended Consequences

> ➤ Enabling online social interaction between strangers made room for trolls to emerge. So we create things like CivilComments.com to overcome the consequences and still benefit from the technology.

PART FOUR:
CULTIVATE—ONGOING ITERATION

CHAPTER 8:

EVALUATION AND ITERATION

The Ongoing Cultivation of Flows

"Each step is always the first step." One of the practitioners we met uses this short sentence to teach people how to deal with change. The explanation is simple but highly motivating.

"Yes there is a goal we try to achieve, yes there is a plan how to get there, but as soon as you have accomplished the first step your ecosystem has changed. Not only because the world is not static, but even more so because you have taken this step: you have acted, so your environment has reacted, or is preparing to react. The reaction may be predicted, or a surprise to you, may offer new opportunities, or block a path you had envisioned in your plan. Therefore you need to treat the next step as a new first step: look around, observe and adapt your plan. We all need to do that, because a reaction may manifest itself anywhere, may only be noticeable to you. It is a shared responsibility to gather that intelligence and adapt your path."

Seeing the world as interconnecting flows makes this obvious.

Agile Software Development is another implementation of this observation. It offers a way to develop software that is responsive to what is being learned in the act of making, along with adapting to client feedback.

What makes something a set of flows rather than a hierarchy of static entities is that they change. Iteration matters as you adapt to changing conditions. However, you should not also be tossed on the waves of change. In this chapter we suggest paths to help you approach fluidity and responsiveness with an idea and organization. The internal structure and processes evolve in order to continue to reflect and engage the external environments in which they are situated.

At this point, the original design has been made and tested, the tools like "Current-Sees" are in use, and the flow starts to be shaped. We all know that the evolution of our social organisms does not stop. And there is no such thing as "changing only one variable while everything else stays the same." Even the introduction of a single new process or tool—and the change of flows that results—will lead to new and unforeseen reactions and effects that might, in turn, require an adjustment.

The first time the new idea hits the street can be exciting and scary at the same time. By engaging more and more people during the previous phases a lot should be known already; there should already be a lot of fans supporting the flow. But as your flow grows, it will cause a reaction in your environment. Remember the example of Lean and Green in Chapter 1: a first success will create a counter reaction.

The trick is to use feedback to adapt and to cultivate the flow. This chapter explores feedback, how to harvest it, assess and reflect on it, how to think through the creation of instruments to collect feedback, along with some lessons from practitioners on ways to adjust flows that might be different than how we approached mechanistic organizations.

We have neatly placed this chapter after Operationalizing. However, as mentioned earlier, the linearity of the book is nothing like the real practice, which is messy and recursive. When working with living, flowing ideas and organizations, we must always be taking in feedback, learning from it, and adapting. We may adapt our way of navigating the new territory, our structure, our processes and governance, or the ways we use technology to support our endeavors. While in some ways, this is the most critical element of flows—to be responsive, evolving, and adapting—we had to have something to work with before we could discuss ways to get feedback on it.

Feedback

The language of a project manager is geared towards managing deliverables and reaching milestones, ticking boxes. For someone who is cultivating flows, it is all about getting feedback, about understanding how your collective actions have changed your environment and how you need to adapt. You operationalized the new idea, and its purpose is to have an effect on flows in an ecosystem. Trying to predict beforehand all the likely consequences is neither productive nor possible, so fast and appropriate feedback is vital.

Feedback includes any information gathered to assist in shaping the flow. It doesn't just come directly. Forecasting or running future scenarios is also a form of early feedback. Surveying our stakeholders about their preferences is a form of active, pre-emptive intelligence-gathering.

One result of the reframing and navigating process is that you developed a follower base and an intelligence network of knowledgeable participants and other interested people. In the very early phases, when the reframe and the narrative are young, you will attract, most likely, only people who are really committed to it, who put something of themselves into the process. It pays to keep them in the loop, to acknowledge them and their contribution, to share intelligence with them, to ask them to help with indirect information-gathering. These people continue to be sensors of the flow. Continue to engage with your network in collecting, assessing, and acting on feedback.

Harvesting

Once you have collected feedback, harvest it by evaluating and integrating it into next steps. Make sense of the information gathered. Harvesting means combining direct feedback and the observations of participants and of the intelligence network in an ongoing assessment of your flow's status. The more people in the core who can share observations and discuss scenarios, the better the harvesting cycle is and the stronger the group becomes. In _Social Physics: How Good Ideas Spread_, Alex Pentland shows that success at innovating requires us to go through cycles of designing and testing the design against other sources of feedback. The feedback is evaluated and integrated to start a new cycle. Those groups that harvest the most feedback from these cycles, and make progress as a result, outperform others. In this mindset, even disappointments are opportunities to learn and correct, provided you harvest as much knowledge as possible.

Any reaction that you witness is new information, new intelligence. It tells you something about your assumptions: which are correct and which need to be added or changed. You can test your scenarios and contingency plans with new intelligence or tweak your structure, protocols, governance, and technology. Or you can assess the reactions of flows, and the reaction of forces and interests that have different priorities in mind. A bit of paranoia goes a long way towards protecting your flow.

These reactions tell you something about the forces that want to limit the growth of the new flow, or want to get control over its development. The old maxim "first they ignore you, then they ridicule you, then they fight you, then you win" expresses how action begets reaction.

Harvesting also means keeping on course: the trap to look out for when gathering so much external intelligence is that all the waves and headwinds seem to demand an immediate reaction. Some do, most of them do not. Part of harvesting is selecting which feedback to respond to and which to discard. Your compass is the narrative that guides the development; your sensory equipment and metrics tell your group whether you are keeping to your course. And all the external noise and actions can be seen as reflections of your own progress.

Reflection

Being 'inside' the core membrane because you are committed to maintaining security and safety, and caring for each other, matters now more than ever. Together, reflect on what the feedback that has been harvested means and how to then adjust the course. It may feel vulnerable to assess ourselves, but if we maintain security, safety, and care, we can process the information gathered to make wise decisions for our next steps.

In the longer run, self-reflection is a vital ingredient of cultivating and growing the flow. Different processes and structures are suited to different reflection cycles as well. Different layers of the membrane of an entity may have different cycles for reflection. Where is the reflect and reset phase? We didn't find, in practice, any hard rules about when to reflect. It is an art to reflect at the appropriate time and about the appropriate process or structure.

This work is always a work in progress. Flows are in motion, dynamic, and changing. The act of getting a flow started triggers the development of progressive insight, generating new ideas, new demands. The context is changing independently, so we need our designs to also be in constant flux, to adapt and evolve. This is something that must be built into the design of the governance, and that may even be forced through, against the natural tendency to become complacent. For example, to fight complacency, we could create forced expiration dates that require quite deliberate actions and efforts if an old structure or design is to be maintained. We might create a Current-See and find that people hoard it, so we need to force it to decay in value if it is not circulating (while using it resets the timer).

Donella Meadows points out very clearly that the timing of feedback loops matters to the stability of a system. Too much latency, too much delay, and we may wander way off course, requiring brutal course corrections. Being too quick to react may have other dangers, creating chaotic behavior and loss of stability. In a process hierarchy, one may distinguish different critical timescales at various levels: very quick feedback at the operational levels, slow at strategic level, so the timing of feedback loops may differ. Allow membranes to find their appropriate feedback cycle.

So how do you iterate in the complex social landscape, using an evidence-based approach? How can you keep going deeper? What else do you need to consider? What about the ethics of the system? How do you improve your ability to sense, design, test, and scale the system appropriately?

There are very few hard and fast rules. There is no cookbook full of tried and true replicable recipes. You are never "swimming in the same river" so how do you continue to experiment wisely? How do you design the system to check, measure, reflect, and adapt over time? How are you collecting data to inform decision-making? While there are no hard rules, there are good tools. We will explore ways to answer these questions in the sections below.

Tools for Hacking Flows

Action Spectrum as a Tool for Iterating

The <u>Action Spectrum</u>, introduced in Part 1, helps make some sense of the layers of time or scope. Remember the Action Spectrum is three overlapping zones. The innermost is the realm of what you can control. The next is what you can guide or influence. And the outer zone is what you can nurture.

One of the defining characteristics of the Nurture zone is that the complexity is so immense that we can't unpick how causality functions there. It is unpredictable. Causality might not even make sense as a way to think about it. Causality is only clear in the Control zone. Our assessments need to reflect this difference between the layers. So when we are collecting feedback, it can help to look for indicators that what we control is giving us the result we want. But we also need to look at indicators that what we nurture is possibly (but not certainly) creating the conditions for what we want to have happen.

We can also look at these zones in terms of time. We have more control over what is happening in the short term, while we can only guide medium term, and at best we can nurture the long-term results we want. We want to know the future, but the best we can do is set off in the direction we want and reach destinations that are near to us. We call this "destinations or directions" because we can plan, in the short term with our allies, for a destination near to us, but we can only contribute toward the long-term direction we want to go in, since the world is changing too much for us to know what that destination will even be like when we get closer. These destinations and directions are another way of sorting feedback. Does this feedback tell me I have arrived where I want to be at this point? Does this feedback let me know I am going in the direction I want to go in?

We can look at the Action Spectrum zones as rings in the network or layers of membranes. We control ourselves, we guide others on our team or through agreements, and we nurture the organization or ecosystem. We can work with these zones when we are gathering feedback as well: information we have, our collaborators have, and the ecosystem as a whole. We could relabel them: me, we, all. Again, we can use this with feedback. Does the information let me know that I am doing the right thing? Does it tell me whether we, together, are making progress? And does the information let me know that as a whole all of us are closer to the vision we share?

Metrics on 'control' often differ from metrics on 'guide' or 'nurture' actions. 'Control' is likely to be clear and measurable, and feedback will come quickly. 'Guide' may be more complicated, more difficult to attribute, and harder to measure because it is collaborative. Feedback for what we are nurturing is often qualitative and more difficult to attribute to our actions without subjective testimony. Often indicators for 'nurture' are ecosystem-wide rather than traceable to our own actions, so coordinating with others in the ecosystem to gather and refine this feedback can be helpful.

Let's say you are working with Virtual Reality, then the thing you are trying to nurture might be a shift in general social perception of the technology, to popularize it. Your project may not be the only one working on this issue, so surveys reporting on the shift in public perception will not only be the result of your efforts. Similarly, if your organization is working to end homelessness, you may have very specific indicators for your program's results with the people you engage, but the broader issue of ending homelessness is most likely something that many organizations are bringing different tools and approaches to in your community. Teasing apart whose program is making the biggest difference may be immensely complex. Seeing if progress is being made overall is not. Cooperation with other players in the ecosystem can be enormously helpful in gauging whether collectively you are making advances on the vision to popularize VR or end homelessness, etc.

Use the Action Spectrum as a framework to orient the feedback you are harvesting, if you want to cultivate flow.

Assessment

We have talked about feedback in general, but for your endeavor you will need feedback specifically suited to your efforts. We interviewed impact assessment expert **Christelle Van Ham** about doing evaluations. She digs into the practice of measurement of the impact of social flows through the creation of metrics to track progress and improve both the impact and the design itself. She took us through the methodical steps listed briefly here:

- ➢ Clarify Purpose and Scope
  - Why do the assessment? Is it to feed your strategy, improve quality, or tell a better story (internally or externally)?
  - Who is the target audience for the evaluation? What do they want? (This will help determine the scope and quality of the evaluation as well.)
    - o Does your audience want to feel something (progress, empathy, belonging, validation, etc.) or do they need specific recommendations for action?
  - Time. How far are you into the project and how much time can you put into evaluating it? If you are just starting, you can begin to collect data for comparison over time, whereas if the effort has been long-term, comparative data may be limited to subjective story-telling now.
  - Resources. What skills, budget, and capacity do you have to do an evaluation? Right-size your evaluation plan to the time, money, and skills you have or can hire.

- ➢ Refine methods and measures (the next section on Instrumentation can help develop more clarity on what to look for in this set).
  - Generate impacts or outcomes of the endeavor. Then refine that list to five to ten impacts or outcomes that will be the most useful ones to track for the audience being served. Consider, in that refinement, what information you have or will already produce. Which outcomes are common, valued, and can be attributed to your effort?
  - Indicators. For outcomes that are not already supported by good information, what would serve as strong indicators?
  - Reliable methods. Collect information on the indicators you have identified using reliable methods and a standardized language and process. This may reduce the ten desirable outcomes to five that you can actually get objective data on.

> ➤ Leave room to modify and evolve the evaluation process as you move forward.

- • Implement.

Doing assessment well depends on many factors, not only the outcomes we want to track. It also depends on the information that we have collected, the resources we have for reflection and assessment, what information flows we share and receive from others, and how long we have been collecting information consistently.

Be sure to track multiple indicators, as single indicators can lead to achieving goals while decimating our values, for example. Remember, people are not always motivated by the same things. If your indicators are only financial, they will only motivate those who are drawn to money. Consider what indicators can reveal social wellbeing in the group, so that those motivated to hold the collective together also have a sense of belonging.

Hypothesis and Instrumentation

Once you have indicators that you want to collect feedback around, then you have to develop ways to gather information on them. We call this step instrumentation. The instruments to use for gathering information can vary widely. Maybe we have a sensor to count how many people walk into a store, or track where they walk in a market. It is exciting to have all these sensors, but we need to be sure we are gathering the right information to test for our desired outcomes. The most important step in instrumentation is being very clear on the hypothesis.

Let's say that we are interested in shifting the social dynamics of the office space. We want to encourage collaboration after getting feedback that most collaborations were happening outside the office during lunch because the office was not conducive to it. How do we create sensors to test for collaboration? We have first to get clear on what it means to be collaborative. How would we recognize it? After a lengthy debate, we decide that collaboration means people taking turns talking with roughly equal inputs from all parties. We can build instruments to track voice patterns in our space to see if these turn-taking conversations happen there. We may also measure a space that we know to be collaborative, to see if this indicator is appropriate as well as tracking other types of conversation to see if this hypothesis fits.

Thomas John McLeish, Director of Experience Technology and Emerging Analytics at Sapient Nitro, describes the process of designing "big data" instrumentation to test our hypothesis about social flows. He builds sensor-based ethnographies around models and hypotheses of how something works for people. His method augments traditional ethnography techniques by incorporating new approaches made possible by distributed sensing, massive data storage, and increasingly sophisticated algorithms (machine learning or clever statistics). What has changed in the last decade is that we have a deeper ability to measure, on a granular level, various physical activities. The world is filled with sensors, something our forefathers did not have and therefore never considered in their designs. We have to invent ways to deal with this new-found flow of feedback, both in harnessing the potential benefits and mitigating risks.

To do this work well, we have to ask rich questions and refine our hypotheses. One of the metrics of a good question is how many questions it generates in response. McLeish says, "Put yourself in the position of an alien—how do I get outside existing expectations? How do I escape the culture I am embedded in with the assumptions it is already operating within? How do I cultivate the alien view?"

To accomplish this, he and his colleagues use four different techniques:

> *How and Why:* keep asking the how or why question, with child-like curiosity, of each explanation given.

> *Basic Word Games:* keep asking what each part of the high-level description means until you get to something usefully measurable as an answer. For example, "What does innovation mean here?"

> *How would you know:* similarly, refine the "what is that?" question with "how would you know?" to get to the things you can build measures and instruments for.

> *Concept Maps:* use idea bubbles with connectors and or overlaps (Venn) to make maps that connect the question to the things you associate with it.

They often mix and match methods to come up with a more holistic understanding of the question being asked and how it connects to what they can create instruments for and measure. For his clients, McLeish then takes the question, creates the instruments to test for it, runs the experiment, and then produces multi-dimensional visualizations of the resulting information.

Beware the allure of new types of instrumentation. Just because you could find a use for a sensor does not mean it will be valuable to do so. Work to get clarity on what needs to be sensed so that the instrument fits the indicator. The trick to truly effective instruments and the useful data that comes from them lies in the clarity of the hypothesis.

Sample Flow Hacks from Practitioners

Self-Steering Metrics

In Chapter 6 we gave the example of the self-steering metric devised by the owner of Randstad, allowing for good and quick feedback to see if actions had the desired effect.

Choosing the wrong metric has the opposite effect. A regional hospital had put "hospitality" on top of its list of objectives. The patients were guests, visiting the hospital to receive care. Being ill is bad enough in itself, and visiting a hospital should be as pleasurable as possible. Everybody agreed that this was the right idea and that it would lead to innovations and improvements.

Management organized a workshop for themselves with external consultants and moderators. After two days of brainstorming and filtering ideas, they selected (amongst others) the idea of making the main reception area less formal, more like at home. Interior decorators were invited to pitch their ideas in a contest. Unfortunately, the cost of implementing the really good interior designs was prohibitive, and the affordable solutions, in the opinion of most managers, just didn't cut it. Frustration started to build, and at one point it was decided to stop the project: better not to change anything than to throw money at a solution nobody liked. A lot of money spent, and a lot of enthusiasm wasted.

If this had been framed as a challenge to design for social flow, a different approach might have been taken. The first question is what value the patient gets from a hospital, and how social flows can enhance that value. Let's define a patient as someone who is feeling unhealthy compared to normal. Normal is a subjective and age-dependent condition; unhealthy can be defined as "when you cannot function as you are used to doing when you are what you think of as normal." Being unhealthy can have a secondary effect on your family, friends, and work: they may feel the negative effects as well on their lives as you cannot function as expected.

You allow doctors, nurses and other carers to invade your life, body, and privacy to correct your "unhealthiness." They are guests in your life and body. The value you receive should be a combination of reducing the "distance to normal" and minimizing the length of time that you feel "unhealthy." The quicker and the closer you get to normal, the better the service is.

Research by Valarie Zeithaml et al. on how people define quality dimensions of service shows that we rank five dimensions of quality in order of priority:

1.	Reliability (defined as predictability)
2, 3, 4=	Customization, Responsiveness, Empathy
5.	Look-and-feel

Spending time and money on interior decorating is clearly work on the least important factor—a hygiene factor but not the one where you make a difference.

Designing for social flow could mean improving the service so that you get better as soon as possible and return as far as possible to your "normal" with the smallest possible impact on your friends, family, and work. The medical procedures needed to cure you may follow a standard protocol, while the arrangement by which you restore your life back to "normal" may be highly customized.

The metric could be twofold:

➢ Measuring the time it takes to get back to "normal" per patient.

➢ Measuring the reduction of the effects of not being in the "normal" state per patient.

These kind of metrics would be very revealing and important to everybody in the hospital. They would pinpoint problems immediately and help in sustaining efforts to improve the patient's condition.

More Current-Sees

Money talks, because it can be counted and traded. But it does not tell everything we need to know; it often gives misleading metrics. **Arthur Brock** says:

"Money and its accounting practices have led us to believe that the things we easily measure with dollars are "tangible" and things not so easily bought and sold are "intangible." A deeper look casts doubt on this conclusion. Under general accounting, **sources of all value** are not actually valuable (like health, ingenuity, trusted relationships, well-functioning teams, the fertility of nature, etc.) only their **saleable by-products** have value (like drugs, patents, purchases, labor, products, crops, commodities, etc.). By what a currency measures and fails to measure it wires a particular pattern of awareness into our businesses, governments and institutions."

Creating a good metric for the flow that you are designing and implementing (or its effect) is a great help in sustaining the effort, especially in a corporate setting. The same can be said about alternative currencies in the sense that Brock describes "Current-Sees" in his essay.

These "Current-Sees" make a flow visible and countable because they *isolate* the exchange from generic money. The isolation is the first benefit. Take for example the token used for trading places in a queue: the flow becomes possible because tokens are limited in their use and can have different rules attached to them compared to generic money. The isolation makes them countable and, therefore, suitable as a metric: how many tokens have changed hands? How often are they used? By what percentage of users?

Self-Expiration

One often overlooked tool in the design of flow protocols, processes, and technology is self-expiration. It can be a powerful way to shift a system that needs stimulation. Expirations can be designed to decay or make an abrupt shift.

In the early '90s, Herman Lammers, then Director of Management Development for Océ Technologies NV, made a tour of the corporate world looking for the answer to his question: "what is the key factor for the continuous development of knowledge workers?" Some people keep on developing their skills, wisdom and productivity up to their 70s or later, while others don't. What are the factors that contribute to their continuous development? If there are external factors, can organizations institute a policy that stimulates their development consistently? He wanted to make the tour and ask hard questions now, before corporations began to realize that this knowledge is a competitive factor and closed the door to outsiders.

After a year he came back with the answer: yes, some people have more innate drive than others, but it is external factors like change, new challenges, new relationships, and new knowledge that keep us improving. Building and extending the network of people you know and trust across many different sectors and disciplines is the foundation. They are a rich source of knowledge and experiences to both tap and contribute to.

He operationalized this answer in a simple policy. The rule of thumb is easy: at least once every 3 years you should change one or two (but not three) of the following factors:

> role

> content/subject

> environment

These changes teach staff to adapt to new situations and learn new skills, meet new people, and help prevent them from becoming too routine in their reactions and observations. Faster change can lead to low engagement or trust, and to people failing to witness the results of their actions (a.k.a. not learning), while slower change may lead to resistance to change and irrational fears of the unknown which, in turn, create mental barriers. Keeping one or two factors constant in the change gives people a leg to stand on, value that they can bring to the table while learning the new. The changes enrich the networks of people we know and let us appreciate the relativity of "this is how we do things over here."

Herman Lammers implemented this rule rigorously: project leaders who objected to a prime employee (whom they relied on) being moved away, were told that they should have a contingency plan in case their star performer suddenly got ill. That might happen very abruptly, so what's the problem if you get three months' warning of their departure?

If the right change could not be offered inside the company, he openly discussed with employees the option of them gaining experience outside the company, and coming back later in a subsequent career step.

This was an excellent operationalization of a profound idea in a corporate context. But if people need this constant rejuvenation, how about the organizations we design and use? How about laws we design? Shouldn't they be renewed and evolve over time?

For example, the wealthy creator of a foundation or a trust will usually have had a sharp and well-focused idea of what the foundation should accomplish. But who can foresee what will be wise 30 years or more in the future? That is usually left to a board of trustees, who may include descendants of the founder. A foundation only has to pay out about 5% of its wealth every year according to US law. Hence the tendency to focus on generating more than that 5% in returns from Wall Street so that the trust will continue in perpetuity (including well-paid positions in the board).

Understanding this, even back in the 1920s, Julius Rosenwald created a *spend-down* foundation. It had to deliver all of its funding within 20 years of his death. You may not recognize his name the way you do Carnegie or Rockefeller, although he was just as wealthy (a billionaire in today's dollars). He chose not to put his name on the Museum of Science and Industry in Chicago, although he funded it heavily. He also endowed Booker T. Washington's educational efforts on behalf of black people. He put his wealth (from Sears) into addressing the problems he saw at the time and within a short time after his death. Then the foundation expired.

Built-in expiration dates in laws, structures, and designs would force us to reiterate, reevaluate, and redesign, as an antidote to complacency and stasis. What if instead we have death dates that help encourage evolution of these social organisms?

Inevitably, there is a drawback. Research Analyst Steve Kamman, in our discussions on the topic, noted that built-in expiration dates would create a new breed of rent-seeking entities trying to monetize the upcoming expirations.

It comes down to the big question: what negative side-effects do we accept in order to harvest bigger gains?

Coherence through Evaluation and Iteration

Leadership

Leadership is very important throughout the phases of cultivating social flows. It is a role bestowed by the group on individuals, with the expectation that they will do the right thing to reach the goal set in the narrative. "We take our own role(s) and responsibility, and you look at the total and guide us in the right direction." Leadership is often a role of great trust, sought after by people who desire power. Having formal leadership positions attracts the power-hungry as honey does bears, while informal leadership rises to the occasion. Leadership emerges when some kind of nexus in the form becomes necessary, the ship needs to hold course in changing weather.

In our research on leadership, we were deeply inspired by the work of **Sofia Bustamante and Mamading Ceesay** at London Creative Labs (LCL) which shows how the act of doing creates the foundation for personal leadership. As part of their amazing work in Brixton, South London, they found that, when personal leadership skills are disseminated in the group and embedded amongst key practitioners, then generative effects begin to appear. They can give rise to the kind of distributed leadership that gives continuity and balance, and reduces dependency on those who kickstarted the process. LCL empowers the ones who think they are the bottom of the pile, with no chance. Social Startup Labs were designed by LCL as a Grameen-inspired systemic intervention to reduce poverty—one that both creates new opportunities for work through enterprise and uses that enterprise to address other barriers to employment. Accompanying interventions, such as Skills Camps and Social Startup Incubator, are required to deliver a holistic solution to unemployment.

J *In 2014, I traveled to Thailand for Ci2iglobal's LearnShareConnect Lab in order to connect with others who engage in co-creative social change around the world. We gathered people from 6 continents with a wide variety of co-creative projects to share our lessons and find patterns in co-creation. Using participatory methods, we shared our co-creative projects and learned from each other for 3 days.*

The conversation on leadership focused on how many of our projects encouraged leadership to flow between participants. Perhaps it is more in the nature of co-creation to desire, at least over time, a sense of sharing leadership authority and responsibility. In some cases we found a leader acting more as a facilitator for the group, holding back on their own agenda to help the group surface their own goals and plan. In other cases leadership flowed over the course of a project, where the one with talent or skill in an area would lead that phase of development. We can call these styles participatory leadership, co-creative leadership, flow leadership, or something else altogether; what they seem to share is the fluidity of power—so it doesn't get hoarded—and a sense of power-with rather than power-over others.

While leadership can take many forms and evolve over time, this seems like the core of the social flows leadership approach: to have leadership flow. So it might be that who is leading changes; it might mean leadership is shared or turns taken; it might mean a decentralized, fractal approach to leadership; or it might mean the style of a single leader changes as the entity evolves. Fitness and flow stand out as the core principles.

Defense as a Leader

When you're harvesting feedback, leadership shows up in the way that a leader isn't tossed around by opinions but stays a course. What we saw in practice was the opposite of reactive decisions. Leaders took loud criticism as a sign of going in the right direction. The more another party is criticizing your flow in public, the more people will become aware of its existence— including people who you have not reached yet. Apparently it has become a priority in their minds to try to stop you. It means you have significance.

Trying to bog you down is another strategy that opponents use. Beware of "Greeks bearing gifts" where all kinds of invitations arrive to join committees, talking groups, institutional meetings and so on, to cooperate in reaching a goal for the common good—which may be alluring but are dangerous to your focus. They not only take up your time and energy, but your "representatives" will be invisibly pressed to introduce a hierarchy, not of your own design, in your group. You will be asked to change your plan to fit in with the "common good" plan that already exists. You will be asked to reveal your strategy for the greater good of cooperation. "Experts" emerge, offering their help in getting contacts "higher up," for which they will be the conduit, if only you follow their lead. Beware.

Copycats will emerge if you are successful, able to throw all the resources they save on design and development into marketing to draw attention away from you—inviting you to play their game instead of your own.

Anticipate the critics, inviters, and copycats. Be clear on what is right for the flow, the narrative, and your feedback.

Heretics in a Corporate World

Cultivating social flows in or with a corporation or large bureaucracy runs the risk of being categorized as heresy by orthodox managers, even if the effort is very successful. The orthodoxy, as taught in business schools, builds on the assumption that carrot and stick are required to motivate people, and on a belief in transactional relationships where every exchange is monetized, and in budgets, accounting, and spreadsheets that track the monetized flow. As Bobby Kennedy more or less said, money is easy to count: the trap is to assume that things you cannot count as easily as money do not exist or have value. This is the trap of orthodoxy.

The opposite trap also applies: the assumption that if you *can* count it, it has value. Some companies spend more money on marketing than on labor costs, without having a clear idea of its real value. Marketing spend is easy to count: ads placed, minutes of air time bought, clicks registered, art directors compensated. The value is an enigma, an educated guess at best, only to be estimated after the fact by panels and the like. Yet money is spent lavishly.

There is plenty of research available showing the need for more than orthodoxy can offer. As Dan Pink says, bad things happen to a company when the profit target becomes detached and removed from the purpose motive that engages people. Quality drops, service levels drop, car companies end up with costly recalls, competitors gain market share. Money does not engage people; mastery, autonomy, purpose, and connection/belonging do.

"Air sandwiches" in communication between executives, designers, and their prime customers lead to costly errors in judgment. The value for the company of establishing a social flow between its best users, the experts in applying the product, and corporate executives—a flow that bridges the gap—is immense. The cultivation of social flow, as part of the Social Era, resolves this.

What better advice can you get than from paying customers who use your product every day, who make a living by working with your product or service, who are willing to tell you what is needed to improve or evolve it? They will give this advice for free, because it matters to them. Yet its value is hard to count, as opposed to the costly invoices of expensive consultants.

Cultivating social flows feels like heresy to managers raised in an MBA-style environment, unless those flows are embedded into core metrics endorsed and tracked by top executives. But managers and CFOs have not been taught at school how to fit social flows into the standard accounting metrics. Socials flows do not fit into a command-and-control style of management. So social flows can be scary, hard to explain, and dangerous for your career if they fail or fall out of grace. It takes proactive and sustained endorsement of social flows by top executives to overcome the hesitation, if not outright antagonism, of orthodox managers. The concept of social flows is a remapping and reframing in itself, compared to the current education of management and business administration. As any practitioner knows from experience, some people will immediately warm to such a new idea, some will sit on the fence, and some people will actively oppose any change to the current orthodoxy.

A corporation has its own belief system (a.k.a. culture) which may be contradicted by the new concept. Introducing heresy in a corporation without being burned at the stake requires preparation and tactical moves. There are several possible strategies:

> One important start is to create a good metric for the flow (or its effect). You want to design a metric that gets accepted. That is as important as anything before you start implementing.

> A tangential approach is to measure and seek high-level attention for the costs and severity of the problem, before you try to solve it with social flows.

> A third approach is to seek visible examples of corporations that have implemented something similar, and get their managers to talk about their experience and its effect on their business.

> It pays to get sponsorship from higher up, preferably multiple executives: if you have only one sponsor it gets tricky (subject of turf wars, cleaning the closet by the successor after a change in management, etc.); multiple sponsors give more stability.

If all that fails: accept the fact that culture eats strategy for breakfast and move, seek more fertile ground. There is plenty out there.

Evaluation and Iteration: Conclusion

Our practitioners say that collecting, harvesting, and acting on feedback played an important role in their efforts. LCL started with a hypothesis:

> Providing skills training for under-employed or unemployed people will help them start small businesses.

They learned that people need an empowering worldview in order to use the skills to start a business. So they added coaching, to give their audience an experience of their own value. Edgeryders developed the hypothesis:

> ➤ If we start a self-organizing community of people where those who do the heavy lifting call the shots, they will create solutions and self-regulate.

Which mostly turns out to be true, but gets complicated when the fluid form of the organization has to interact with more traditional entities and processes. So they learned how to adapt to that using greater transparency.

Harvesting feedback, using indicators of progress, and creating the right instrumentation and incentive systems allowed all of our practitioners to continue to adjust course, fitting their environments as they change over time.

Every step is the first step: action begets reaction in an interconnected world, so act and observe. Collect intelligence, harvest the valuable part and adapt your course. Flow is about feeling yourself immersed and connected to relationships and interactions. Harvesting is about selecting what is valuable as well as deciding what is a (deliberate) distraction. The more impact you have, the bigger the counterforces.

Think in 3 levels of influence, and 3 levels of time: controlling is for achieving short steps, guiding is for holding course in the medium time frame, and nurturing for improving the environment which lets you grow.

The hallmark of great leadership in this process turns out to be choosing your errors and being clear and transparent about what others can expect as we optimize for one thing at the potential expense of another. Holding course in a living, changing environment requires everybody's attention and action: the better the indicators of holding course are, and the more accessible the metrics are for everybody, the more self-steering is seen.

Choose what is important in your goals and accept the errors that are the explicit consequence of any choice. It pays to let everybody accept this trade-off up-front: the trap is to define perfection as a goal.

Heroic efforts in a hostile environment are noble but probably not effective or satisfying: fertile ground is required to plant seeds.

Quick Guide to Evaluation and Iteration

Ongoing Cultivation of Flows

> ➤ Each step is a first step: feedback, reflect, adapt, and iterate.

> ➤ Agile Software Development is a system designed for this ongoing change, for example.

Feedback
What information can we gather about what is happening?

> ➤ Use direct as well as pre-emptive intelligence like forecasting and scenarios, surveying stakeholders.

> ➤ Connect with your follower base and network as sensors of the flow.

> ➤ Actively seek feedback, don't just respond to what returns to you.

Harvesting
How do we make sense of feedback?

> ➤ Evaluate the feedback you get and consciously choose how to integrate it into next steps. Choose your errors.

> ➤ Use your narrative as a compass to guide selection and valuation of the feedback as you harvest.

Reflection
What does this mean?

> ➤ Enable safety, security, and care when processing feedback.

> ➤ How periodically do you reflect and adjust? Meadows says: the timing of feedback loops impacts the stability of the system.

> ➤ Build evolutionary potential into governance and structure.

Tools for Hacking Flows

Action Spectrum as a Tool for Iterating

> ➤ Zones of Control, Guide, Nurture.
>> • layers of causality: causal (simple systems) to unpredictable (complex adaptive systems)

- layers of time: Destinations or Directions
- layers of network: me, we, all

The metrics tend to be different for each layer or membrane.

Assessment

> Clarity of purpose, audience, and scope (time and resources):
>
> - Why do the assessment? Who is it for? What do they need? How much time can be given to it? What resources are available for it?
>
> Methods and measures:
>
> - What outputs or impacts? What outcomes are we trying to show? Which of those are useful for our audience? What information can we or have we gathered to support the claim about those outcomes? How can we attribute those outcomes to our efforts?
>
> What indicators show progress on outcomes and goals?
>
> - What methods enable us to capture information for those indicators? How can we leave room to evolve, such as including more feedback gathering than we can take action on now, so that we can continue to evolve assessment as our resources grow?
>
> Track multiple indicators.

Instrumentation

To use good instruments to feed our indicators, we have to be clear about our hypothesis.

> Beware getting hung up on the latest gadgets for capturing data.
>
> Focus on what you want to track. The key is to ask the best question.
>
> Some tools to help clarify hypothesis are:
>
> - How and why?
> - Basic word games
> - How would you know?
> - Concept maps

Sample Flow Hacks from Practitioners

- ➤ Self-steering metrics
- ➤ Good enough indicators for real-time feedback for everyone at the level of understanding appropriate to them.
- ➤ More Current-Sees
  - Isolate the exchange or flow from money. This helps us track the flow and can be a source of feedback on the flow.
  - Self-expiration: Consider that creating expirations can help avoid stagnation and brittleness.

Leadership for Coherence

- ➤ Leadership in flow is co-creative leadership
  - Encourage everyone in the group to develop leadership skills.
  - Where can leadership flow rather than being hoarded as a form of power-over?
- ➤ Defense as a Leader
  - Beware of gifts and opportunities, while offered with good intentions, they can pull you off course.
  - There will be errors, select which you are okay with and be transparent about it.
  - Criticism is attention, indicates significance. Beware the lure of invitations and being co-opted. Don't compete with copycats on their terms.

Heretics in a Corporate World

- ➤ There are a few ways to support being a heretic
  - Collect good metrics.
  - Clarify and make visible the problem or pain point.
  - Seek examples of the desired shift in peer organizations.
  - Connect with strong sponsors or champions in the organization.

CONCLUSION

We have now looked in detail at each of the steps that we have identified as a necessary part of cultivating social flows. Once you start to explore the ideas and the tools out there that can be applied to the challenges of each step, and perceive them as parts of the whole, a wealth of knowledge opens up. As a result, this book in some ways has really just scratched the surface.

Instead of a regular conclusion we would like to step back and look at one big example which we think will help to pull together the many threads we have explored in these chapters. [We have put phases and key concepts in square brackets to help you navigate the example.]

The Internet

We all use the Internet but relatively few people really understand the conceptual leap driving its success. We conflate the Internet with the services built on top of it, like email, websites, Facebook, Twitter, WhatsApp—as services like these represent the visible value we receive.

Here let's look at the infrastructure that the Internet provides. And let's consider the Internet as being the result, first, of a radical and hugely successful reframe of how you can organize digital data transport, which then went through the stages of navigating and operationalizing until it became so successful it could not be stopped. (Having said that, its huge success means that nowadays governments and global corporations are trying to capture the Internet and control it, or at least control what can be done with it).

Who Owns the Internet?

The radical nature of the Internet becomes apparent when we ask the question "Who owns the Internet?" We are so used to the idea that something has to be owned, by a company or a government, that it is hard to imagine that the Internet is not owned by anyone. It is not.

The physical components of the Internet can easily be identified: the parts are formed by over 26,000 individually owned communication networks (wired and wireless) globally, and exchange points between these networks. The exchange points can be bilateral or for multiple parties like the Amsterdam Internet Exchange [see p.164], or the NYIIX in New York. There are hundreds of IXs in the world. Each network makes its own decisions on how to build and invest, on how to connect to other networks (or not), and how to exchange traffic. To oversimplify somewhat, the Internet is created by the collective of these networks together adhering voluntarily to agreements on address spaces, on how packets of data are formed, on routing packets, on traffic management, and on bilateral agreements on how to exchange traffic. The global Internet emerges from the totality of this cooperation. Because the Internet basically assumes nothing about what data is transported, and requires no permissions to attach a meaning to the data that it transports, it has allowed the creation and widespread adoption of services on top of it. The interpretation of what data in a packet means can be done by sender and receiver—this is the so called "end-to-end" principle. So, creative minds have developed services like email, websites (WWW), VOIP, YouTube, online banking, and so on, by attaching meaning to data.

As we have just seen, there is no single owner of the Internet and there is hardly any formal contract or law for the enforcement of the protocols and agreements that make the Internet a reality. The voluntary adoption of agreements has made possible its scale and phenomenal success. Of course some networks tried to modify the agreements and create a walled garden. But cutting their subscribers off from the wealth that was growing outside of it created an outcry that reversed that process, cementing adherence to wider agreements.

The Internet is a big, hairy, audacious idea about how to let independent networks cooperate to make something much bigger, something emerging from the cooperation, something beyond their individual reach.

And that idea relied upon another radical departure from accepted wisdom: the idea that unpredictable, governed-by-chance, no-guarantees-beyond-"best effort", data transport is better suited to our needs than controlled and predictable data circuits.

Choosing Your Errors

Before 1960 the standard method of electronic communication required setting up a circuit between two hosts that wanted to communicate: like the telephone switchboard, where someone "plugged you in" and created a direct and exclusive channel for you and your counterpart (the Bell System). Or with radio, leading to the famous "Over!" shouted into microphones when you signaled to the other party that they could send while you received, using the same frequency. A circuit is a predictable and controlled thing, top-down managed.

Telephone companies controlled the voice network. You asked for a circuit, they let you know if capacity was available and how much, and it was reserved (and billed) for you on request. Governments allocated (and monetized) radio frequency-bands for particular uses. (So the term "bandwidth" came from allocating radio frequencies: the wider the "band" of frequencies you were allocated, the more capacity you had available.) If the available capacity was fully used, bad luck, you had to wait until somebody relinquished a circuit. But hey, it was a tremendous improvement on sending letters. Huge (profitable) companies, often state monopolies, were created to service this demand.

Private data networks were built on the same idea: you allocated capacity on demand to a (virtual) circuit between two endpoints and made it fully available to users, even if they transported nothing. Data networks prided themselves on their reliability.

Complete predictability was chosen as the most important quality to strive for. Predictability required top-down control and this meant a trade-off. As a result, innovation was limited severely, a lot of capacity was wasted capacity, and prices were forced up.

It is hard to imagine now how utterly heretical the new idea of packet-switched networks must have been in those days. First of all, packet-switched networks throw the idea of reserved circuits out of the window and replace it with the idea of statistical multiplexing of a structured set of bits, called a "packet," over a transmission line. Statistical multiplexing is something we do every day, driving on the highway, sharing the capacity of the road. Setting up a circuit (the old idea) on a road would be equivalent to reserving a complete lane from where you ramp up to where you exit, just for you alone. It's obvious in this example how wasteful that method would be in traffic. So we share the available capacity, based on the observation that each of us only needs a part of the capacity of the road every now and then. Only seldom does our actual combined demand exceed the capacity of the road (leading to traffic jams), which is a small price to pay compared to the alternative.

The second idea packet-switched networks are based on is that the network topology (what routes and interconnections there are) and network state (is everything working? are there jams?) is globally unknown and only locally known. Each packet is sent and finds its own path to the destination, maybe arriving out of sequence. There isn't even any guarantee that the packet will arrive at all: it may disappear along the route. How does that work? It's like driving on roads: there are many roads leading to Rome because they are interconnected by junctions. A free-form network will have many connections and junctions (routers) that give the option of many paths to a destination. How do you find your path if you do not have a map? When your packet arrives at a junction (router) the router inspects the destination address and sends the packet to the next junction/router where the process is repeated. The decision about what branch to take is based on two pieces of information: can your destination address can be reached through that branch, and how busy is it on that branch? That information is passed back and updated regularly by the upstream routers that are connected. (These routers get their information from their peers as well, and so on until an endpoint is reached.) If there is no route available, or the router is too busy, the packet just gets discarded. Adding a new cable and new routers is easy: once they are powered up they advertise themselves to their neighbors and get information back, and the path and reachable addresses are added in real time. The reverse is also true: if a route or router goes down, the neighbors notice that and adapt. The interesting thing is that none of the routers has to have a complete map of the network to be able to do its job; it only needs local knowledge. Unlike roads, the Internet does not have a map, nor is a map needed for it to function.

[Reframing and Navigating]

The big reframe in the 1960s was to apply this idea of statistical multiplexing to electronic digital communication between computers, observing the fact that most communication is very "bursty": short periods of intense exchange of data interspersed by periods of silence.

Packet-switched networks reversed the trade-off. Now very effective use of capacity and permissiveness of innovation were valued more highly than predictability and control.

While the idea was laughed away by the big telecom and computer companies, DARPA (the US Defense Advanced Research Projects Agency) funded research into the possibilities of packet-switching because it held the promise of more resilient communication networks in times of war and destruction. RAND corporation (Paul Baran) came up with the concept of packet-switched, store-and-forward networks. Centralized, top-down controlled communication networks are vulnerable to attacks that take out the control centre, while packet-switched networks do not have a central control centre and can therefore adapt to outages in some sections of the network.

The idea was adopted by Donald Davies (NPL) in the UK and put into reality. He made the first practical implementations possible, starting the navigation phase where multiple teams began to tinker away.

These first practical implementations in Europe and the USA showed researchers the possibilities of the idea, and allowed them to find solutions to problems that arose in practice—breaking new ground in the process. An example was the work of Louis Pouzin in France, implemented in the CYCLADES network. The most important legacy of CYCLADES was the proof that moving the responsibility for reliability of the communication (traffic management and integrity of data) out of the network into the end-points did actually work, against all the received wisdom. Computers that communicated with one another compensated for an unreliable and unpredictable network between them, and the combination produced a well-functioning service.

The concept of CYCLADES became a cornerstone in the design of the Internet. Data transmission was a state monopoly in France at the time, so special dispensation was needed to run the CYCLADES network. The French PTT did not agree to the government funding a competitor to their (circuit-based) data network, and insisted that the permission and funding be rescinded. By 1981, CYCLADES was forced to shut down. But many other experimental networks were built and used by research groups and universities. [**Navigation**]

DARPA, however, could ignore the pressure from commercial interests which did not like any competition to their proprietary network designs. DARPA funded the development of the experience gained by many teams into a standardized scalable definition of packet-switched inter-networking. Between 1973 and 1982 the results of much research were embedded, tested, codified, and published (like the famous RFC 675, Cerf and Kahn, in December 1974). The core group of experts who guided the standardization process consistently held onto the key idea of the reframe and resisted attempts to weaken the concept. [**Immune system, Emergent Scaling as a strategy**]. They had little idea how successful and scalable it would soon become.

[Operationalizing and Scale]

Deliberately designing for an unreliable network was heresy to the incumbents: they prided themselves on exquisite, predictable reliability, and were accustomed to the benefits (power and financial) of central control.

What they did not see, but DARPA, researchers, and universities did, were the huge benefits:

> ➤ The simplicity of the routing design reduced greatly the complexity of the packet switches (routers), making this type of networking vastly cheaper, and thus attractive to cash-strapped universities and startups.

> ➤ You could tinker as much as you liked without bringing the network down, again highly attractive for universities and startups, leading to an accelerated innovation cycle.

> ➤ You could add capacity, add new routes, and make new connections without asking anybody for permission, at any time.

> ➤ You also didn't need permission to invent and implement a new service.

And, for the military, the promise of a resilient network that could not be decapitated in times of war became a reality.

In 1984, the US Defense Department made TCP/IP[5] the standard for all military networking, giving it a position no commercial interest from telephone companies or computer companies could ignore or squash. **[Endorsement and backing]**

The "inter-networking" part of the Internet Protocol Suite defined how various independent networks could cooperate in transmitting data between two endpoints, each on different networks. This feature was quickly adopted by universities and researchers wanting to share information, spreading to startups and companies as university graduates

---

[5] TCP/IP (Transmission Control Protocol and Internet Protocol) has become the shorthand for the codified and standardized definition of packet-switched (inter-) networking. TCP is the cornerstone for traffic management and relies on the receiver to send an ACK (acknowledgment) back to the sender for each packet received. The neat trick is that TCP increases the speed of sending until it starts to notice missing ACKs: a packet is dropped somewhere, or delayed too long. TCP reduces speed and resends the missing packets. After a while it slowly increases the sending speed until it starts to notice missing ACKs again, and so on, adapting in real time to unknown conditions. In this case, the error (dropping packets) becomes an essential feature.

started their careers. The fact that each individual network could interconnect on its own terms, and with networks it chose (or not), turned out to be key to the suite's adoption.

[In our terminology: groups were free to gather their resources around their own purpose and become their own entity, with their own internal flows, in the form they desired—so long as they agreed to the standards for inter-entity flow of data, the address space, and how to interconnect: the agreements of flow on the next emergent level.]

Independent governance bodies were formed to distribute knowledge and incorporate new features into new standards. [**Governance, operationalizing**]

The Interop trade show allowed companies to demonstrate their new products to potential customers, spreading adoption. [**Scaling**]

Researchers meanwhile happily created services to make their life easier: like chat, file transfer, email, and browsing. The World Wide Web was created in 1989 by Tim Berners-Lee at CERN to meet the demand for automatic information-sharing between scientists in universities and institutes around the world, on thousands and thousands of computers. Famously, the creators offered the idea to many large telecom and computer companies for monetization, but nobody was interested. It took the creation of the first good browser, MOSAIC, in 1992 and its commercial descendant, Netscape Navigator, in 1995 to show the potential of the idea outside the military and universities. The rest is history.

[Evaluating and Iterating]

In hindsight the key role of DARPA in funding and supporting the vulnerable navigation and operationalizing phases can hardly be underestimated. The subsequent success in scaling up and out has taken everybody by surprise and has shaken up many industry segments. At the same time, new downsides have become apparent: extremely cheap and intrusive state-surveillance, exposure to new types of warfare, network effects that create new monopolies, and the dark side of humanity has been augmented as well as the good side. Some fear that connecting all devices to the Internet will become a nightmare of security risks.

We are in the middle of huge struggles to find new solutions to these new challenges, where some parties would like to return to central control. Net Neutrality is a prime example of the battle between these ideas and reframes.

The story has only just started; this is the first big reiteration.

Afterword: Invitation to Engage in Cultivating Social Flows

Writing this book made us see that there are so many practitioners and thinkers who are working alone or in small networks, without realizing that they could be part of a much larger group.

We have created a website: first, to make more and more learning and work accessible to others, and secondly to support a community of practitioners. Please look over the website and contribute!

This is an emergent field—designing for the strengths of people and leveraging technology to enable us to be more productive together. Please join us in exploring, sharing, and iterating this field.

This book is a reframe and the first deliverable for us. We invite you to help us iterate. We circle back using our own process to flow with you for our next prototype. Join us at CultivatingFlows.com to continue.

ABOUT THE AUTHORS

Jean M. Russell is a culture hacker, facilitator, and writer on a quest to catalyze group productivity. As a founder of the Thrivability movement, Jean works with change agents, innovators, and new economy builders, globally, through the Thrivable Futures Consultancy.

In 2013, Jean published *Thrivability: Breaking Through to a World That Works* with Triarchy Press. She received an honorable mention on the Enrich List as one of the top 200 people enriching our path to a sustainable future. She is also listed as one of 100 women globally co-creating a P2P Society. In 2010, with 65 inspiring people, she curated, *Thrivability: A Collaborative Sketch* which has been seen by well over 30,000 viewers. She has published articles on organizational design strategies, and her work on thrivability, innovation, philanthropy, and cultural shifts has been highlighted in *The Economist, Harvard Business Review,* and *Stanford Social Innovation Review.*

Since 2007, she has been facilitating strategy retreats, conferences, and workshops in North America, Europe, and Australia. She brings to her facilitation a keen understanding of social network analysis, motivation and behavior patterns, group dynamics, and culture change. Jean often custom designs participatory structures for group engagement that evoke play to achieve purpose.

She loves hiking to Tennessee Valley Beach for a picnic with some Vinho Verde, crusty rustic bread, and a selection of cheese so she can savor the flavors while watching crepuscular colors shift on sand and water at sunset.

Herman E. Wagter is an independent program manager specializing in complex collaborative innovation programs, where technical innovation needs to be combined with social innovation to get the desired impact. He supports customers by developing and refining a comprehensive strategy to achieve the desired goal, as well as by leading the subsequent iterative implementation phases hands-on. One example is the public-private venture to kickstart Fiber-to-the-Home in Amsterdam, including the successful discussion with the European Commission on the application of the Market Economy Investor Principle regarding the role of the Municipality of Amsterdam. Another is the strategic development of the Lean & Green movement aimed at increasing the competitiveness of companies through the voluntary reduction of CO_2 emissions during the transport of goods.

In his early career as Managing Director in international contracting and services he became interested in the social dynamics of change and the role of social technology in shaping how we work together. As a practitioner who is keen on what creates impact he continuously searches for knowledge, ideas, and experiences to apply in his work. That search includes legal issues like state-aid and public tender processes, new accounting principles, technology, behavioral economics, and human motivation applied to collaboration.

Herman loves to cook for his family, drink good wines with his wife and their friends, and do outdoor sports. He likes to tinker with IT and gadgets and once in a while to enjoy fast mountain roads on his motorcycle.

ABOUT THE PUBLISHER

Triarchy Press is a small, independent publisher of intelligent books and inspiring new ideas about people, organizations and society—and practical ways to apply those ideas.

Thinking about the current omnicrisis and ways to navigate through and beyond it is a feature of many of Triarchy's recent titles:

Jean Russell's *Thrivability* sets out to challenge the 'breakdown thinking' that focuses only on defensive reactions to the economic, social, political, and environmental catastrophes we face. In its place she proposes 'breakthrough thinking': an approach that recognizes the gritty reality but enables us to envision and co-create a world of wellbeing and health.

Graham Leicester's *Transformative Innovation: A Guide to Practice and Policy* is a stand-alone guide to realizing transformative potential at scale— for policymakers, funders, and innovators outside the commercial sector.

Jonathon Porritt calls Daniel Wahl's *Designing Regenerative Cultures* "an extraordinary intellectual and analytical resource, providing as good a picture of contemporary holistic, systems-based thinking as you're likely to find."

Nora Bateson's *Small Arcs of Larger Circles* is a foray into "unauthorized knowledge." In a series of essays, conference talks, stories, quotes and poems, she covers linguistics, biology, semantics, cognitive theory, justice awareness, and embrace of paradox.

Patricia Lustig's *Strategic Foresight* is a practical guide to foresight and foresight tools for leaders in business, the public sector and NGOs, to aid their practice in strategy, decision-making, and change.

WWW.TRIARCHYPRESS.NET

CPSIA information can be obtained
at www.ICGtesting.com
Printed in the USA
LVHW052144150723
751920LV00002B/3